# AYNI

*Finding Love, Balance &*
*Harmony*

*For Ourselves, For the World*

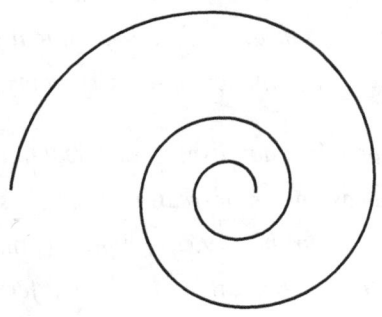

Erin Lucero

First edition

ISBN: 979-8-9878500-1-5

Editing by Carrie Bolin
Cover art by Erin Lucero

This book was professionally typeset on Reedsy.
Find out more at reedsy.com

*In memory of my mother, Joyce.*
*The pain of losing you gave me the courage*
*to go on this journey.*
*Together we heal, so we can at last,*
*become butterflies.*

# Contents

# Foreword

We all know that magical scene in the Wizard of Oz when a young Dorothy, having just looked death square in the eye after being swept away by a terrifying tornado, steps out of the rubble of her old house to see her entire world transform from black and white to colour.

As she opens the door, a sombre sky as grey as weeping angels is replaced by an ocean of colour, delicious heaven-sent music, flora of every creed and colour and birds singing joyously in the trees. The tornado has shifted her from 3D to 5D into a brand new world illuminated by the soul of summer; a place overflowing with peace, tranquility, balance and harmony.

It is a land we all dream of visiting one day; and a place we all have access to if we are given the guidance and are willing to take every decision with courage.

For Dorothy, this was the moment of her great awakening; the humble beginnings to an epic journey where she will soon find courage, brains, heart and, ultimately, herself along the way.

Now, keeping Dorothy and her incredible journey in mind, take a deep breath and have a look at where you are in your life right now.

There may not be a tornado or hurricane in your midst, a pair of magic red shoes hugging your feet, or even a fresh coat of paint on a yellow brick road to whisk you off toward your holy grail.

There is, however, this exquisite little book called 'Ayni', written by Erin Lucero which you have just 'coincidentally' picked up and opened which contains every single step you need to take along your own yellow brick road.

Erin introduces us to the Medicine Wheel and four ancient archetypes, known in the Andean shamanic world as power animals, all of whom walk beside you as you begin to step into your power and transform your life. Step aside tinman, lion, scarecrow, and wicked witch as the lineage usher in the magic of the serpent, mother/sister jaguar, royal hummingbird, and the eagle/condor.

Having spent some quality time with this book over the last month, I can promise you that IF you are willing to read it from cover to cover and bathe in the wisdom, embracing it with absolutely every ounce of your being, your spiritual GPS system will take you by the hand and steer you all the to the Emerald City living deep in your heart. Or, put another way, you will find 'Ayni'.

The first time I set eyes on Erin, I knew she was extraordinary.

Before me sat this beautiful, wise and courageous soul who was not wholly dissimilar to young Dorothy. Erin had just stepped out of her own personal hurricane, having lost her mother in her physical form and, like all of us when we lose one of the mainstays in our life, felt like her world had been turned upside down.

But Erin, an architect by trade, saw an incredible opportunity for growth and was determined to rebuild her house and her dreams out of love. And this time, she would let spiritual wisdom and Ayni make this new life construction something very special.

By staying present in the transition of her mother, Erin had witnessed the ultimate truth. Most people's natural instinct is to withdraw from life, run away or suppress their feelings of grief.

Not Erin.

With the help of her partner and her mother who, in her new angelic form, stood steadfastly beside her daughter like a mountain in the sacred valley, Erin was ready to face this hurricane, make peace with it, and begin an epic journey which would soon see her transform this grief into a gift for her and her ancestors and a superpower of monumental proportions to take to the world. Watching her evolve from week to week as she went around the medicine wheel was a joy to witness as her 'teacher' and friend - and the beauty of the story is that her wisdom journey was not just about her. Erin soon turned from student to teacher and this book has now been manifested so that many thousands, and hopefully millions, of people have the opportunity to evolve their souls in the exact same way that Erin did.

This book is YOUR chance to embrace the hybrid of Tantric Yoga and Shamanic wisdom which Erin has so beautifully crafted for us over the pages that follow. It is a masterpiece.

So without further ado, let me step aside, click my shiny red heels together and pass the shamanic baton to my dear sister and wisdomkeeper, Erin.

Yours in Munay,
  Peter


—*P.J. Sanderson is a writer, poet, musician and shaman who is based in France. A former BBC journalist, he was inspired by his journey around the medicine wheel to write the book "The Bird of Destiny: Horus and the Silver Raven," which would raise awareness about climate change and leave a legacy for his children and the seven generations beyond so they can live on a healthier planet.*

# Acknowledgement

First, I want to acknowledge that I live on native lands, and to acknowledge the Indigenous peoples of these lands as the original stewards of this land and all the relatives within it. The tribes of the Ute, Arapaho, Cheyenne, and others, whose ancestral lands are where I now live, have much to teach us about how to live in harmony with Mother Earth. I humbly look to their wisdom and teachings. I acknowledge the part my ancestors played in the taking of their ancestral home and hope to heal and repair our collective home, for all our relations.

I want to give thanks and gratitude to the teachers in life, both formal and informal. Special gratitude to my yoga teachers Svetlana Lambrozo and Swami Muktibodhananda Saraswati for your wisdom and support on my yoga journey, and my shamanic teachers Peter Sanderson and Karen Johnson, and all the teachers of the Four Winds Institute. Peter, who wrote the foreword and introduction for my book, inspired me with his poems and his compassion and gave me the courage to give voice to all these words that lived in my heart. I thank him for sharing and supporting my dream of Ayni, and am full of humble gratitude to Spirit for sending him a new myth about Ayni.

I also acknowledge all those informal teachers, cheerleaders, and supporters. My mother and father were two of my greatest teachers, teaching me strength, compassion, and conviction. It is with great love that I write this book in my mother's memory. I wouldn't be here without the loving support and patience of my husband Eduardo. He has always encouraged me on my journey to self-love and discovery.

He has held me in my grief and my doubts. He's held sacred space with me at fire ceremonies, welcoming in our ancestors and reading the fire. He even had visions of Hummingbird when I was doing my training, his spirit walking alongside mine as I traveled the medicine wheel.

So much gratitude to my sister, and my nieces and nephews, who inspire me to make this world a better place for them, and all the brothers and sisters I have met who share this dream of Ayni. I also want to thank my lifelong friend Natalie Roers, a fellow author and artist, for showing me what it looks like to unapologetically go after your dreams, and encouraging me to write a book and self-publish. Keep living the dream girl!

I kept this book so close to my heart, with very few reading it before it was complete. I want to thank Jessica who gave it the very first read-through, and all her encouragement as I tried out this new role of author. And a huge thanks to my editor Carrie Bolin who helped me cut out some darlings and make the book sing. Their encouragement and positive feedback helped me through all the fears I still held about writing my own book. Also thanks to Joanna Penn who writes amazing self-help books about self-publishing. She made the whole thing seem so easy!

And last, but certainly not least, I want to acknowledge our ancestors and our children's children. We walk along this path because of all those who came before us, and I acknowledge all their struggles and their sacrifices. I heal their wounds as I heal my own so that I can create a better world for our future generations. A world that is full of love and light and Ayni.

In Munay, In Love, In Ayni.

# 1

# Introduction - The Dream of Ayni

I recently traveled to Peru as the culmination of a yearlong or should I say a lifelong journey of my search for love, balance, and harmony. I didn't know what to expect from this adventure—maybe a condor would fly out of the heavens and land on my shoulder or Machu Picchu's stones would whisper to me the great ancient wisdoms. Neither of those things happened, but what I did find was Ayni.

Ayni[1] is an ancient Quechua word from the Andes based on the ideas of giving and reciprocity. It basically means, "Today for you, tomorrow for me." Ayni teaches us that all things are interconnected. If we act today from a place of giving and love for the mutual benefit of all things, then tomorrow the Universe will take care of us. The Universe will always provide what we need, as we are not separate from it. It's a belief that the world is full of abundance and love, not scarcity and fear.

I found Ayni in the Sacred Valley between Cusco and Machu Picchu. Though we were at 10,000 feet above sea level, it was a fertile valley full

---

[1] **AYNI (AY-nee):** A Quechua word, the native language of many of the peoples of Peru, Ecuador, Bolivia, and Argentina. It is best translated as "Today for you, Tomorrow for me." It is also close to the English words reciprocity and mutualism.

of life. The mornings hovered just above freezing, but tropical flowers abounded and hummingbirds zipped around sipping the sweet nectar. The Sacred Valley was full of color, in the flowers, the textiles, and the rainbow flags of the Inca. Everything felt connected and in balance. The forests, the river, and the agricultural terraces seamlessly flowed from one to the next. While I was there, I too came into balance and harmony. I remember sitting on a rock in our hotel's flower garden, closing my eyes, and feeling the warm sun on my face. For the first time in a long time, I felt that everything was exactly as it should be. I felt a deep, heart-exploding kind of love both within myself and for all of the things around me. I felt a calling deep in my soul to begin to live in Ayni. To live in harmony and balance with other people and with nature. It called me to live in a way that is for the mutual benefit of all living things.

While I was in the Sacred Valley, I had several profound dreams. Dreams can be windows into our psyche, and mine had been just itching to come out and talk to me for many months. I want to share one dream with you in particular. This dream is my guiding light, the one that I keep coming back to. It's an invitation to all of humanity, to whoever is also looking for love and balance, and harmony in their own lives.

\* \* \*

*At first, I dreamed of violence. All around me, there was cruel and senseless violence. I called out for people to stop. "Please do something! Please Stop!" I asked myself, "Why isn't anyone doing anything?" But the violence and cruelty only got worse. It was beyond awful. All of the senseless violence in our world in dream form. And I thought to myself in my dream, "I don't want to do this anymore. I am done with this nightmare." And in that exact moment, I realized I was in control of my dreams. So, I said in my dream, "I am done dreaming this!" And the dream ended, and there was darkness.*

*And in the darkness, the question came to me, "Then what do you want to dream?"*

*And I responded, "I want to dream of a world in Ayni."*

*And in the dream, a city began to materialize, a beautiful city with clean streets and buildings of stone with trees and flowers all around. As I walked down the street of this city, others began to join me. They were from all over the world and all walks of life. There were mathematicians and doctors and artists and farmers. And we asked ourselves, how can we all be here? In a shared dream? These were not people I was dreaming up, they were real people, dreaming the same dream as me. Dreaming of a world of beauty and harmony, coming together in community. We asked, "How can this be so?" A little confused and in awe, but so it was. And we knew that we were all meant to be there.*

*Together, we walked down this street, in this beautiful city, in Ayni. I stood out on a balcony, looked around, and saw a beautiful place, a place of peace and harmony, with fields and cities and nature, all connected. I was filled with love and hope and possibility.*

✳ ✳ ✳

I share this dream with you because I know that it can come true. I know we all have this capacity, no matter where we came from or what our story is. We can all come to a place of love, of balance, of Ayni. We can discover this world of harmony, reciprocity[2], and mutualism[3]

---

[2] **RECIPROCITY**: The idea of exchanging things or ideas for the mutual benefit of both parties. Reciprocity is different from a transactional relationship because the fundamental goal is to provide mutual benefit, rather than just an exchange of goods or services.

[3] **MUTUALISM**: This is a term used in biology where two organisms have a relationship and both benefit from the interaction. This would be in contrast to a parasitic relationship.

3

where our actions are for the benefit of all living things.

This book is my journey to finding this within myself, accepting myself heart and soul, and then moving into a place of action for the betterment of all living things. I offer this journey as a roadmap and an invitation for you to also go on your own journey of self-discovery, self-love, and self-actualization. Though our journeys may have many bumps and turns in them, it is truly worth every step. It is the journey out of fear and hopelessness into a place of being in the flow of love and harmony.

For so many years I felt stuck, out of balance, and yearning to find love and light in my life. I heard the call of Mother Nature, saw the beauty in her forests and oceans, but didn't know how to bring that beauty into my own life. I knew the world was out of balance. I knew that I was out of balance. Through the practices of yoga and shamanism, and going on my own great inner journey, I have started to find balance again.

As I came into balance and harmony within myself, I could see how my inner world affected my relationship with others and with the planet. I could see myself mirrored in others' pain and suffering. As I found compassion and love for myself, I could find compassion and love for others, even those I didn't agree with. I could see how our relationship with nature was broken and needed to be fixed. I could hear the whispers of the trees and the wind, encouraging us to come back into right relationship with them. I realized that it wasn't the Earth that was out of balance, it was humanity. It was time for us to examine ourselves, our world, and how we fit into everything.

Feeling stuck and out of balance was a gift for me, because it was my wake-up call to really examine myself, to find love and harmony in my life. If you can relate, I invite you to also go on this journey. When we are in balance, everything flows just as it should. We become unstuck and can find joy and love and happiness in our daily lives, no matter what other people are doing or what comes our way.

It is my sincere hope that as I share my own journey you can see the power of loving ourselves and discovering how we are all interconnected. And in that discovery, you will find love for each other and for the planet. The entire universe is conspiring to help us find unconditional love. I will explore how coming into balance and harmony with ourselves, each other, and the planet will make this world a beautiful and magical place worth living in. I also hope you will feel empowered and inspired to make changes in your own life. Each of us has the power to change the trajectory of the world. We don't need a degree or lots of money, just an earnest desire for change and hearts full of love.

* * *

# AYNI

***

# 2

# Starting the Journey

*"The secret of getting ahead is getting started"*
*–Mark Twain*

Before we jump right to the end, the part where everything is happy and full of butterflies and unicorns, I must say the practices and teachings in this book take a little bit of work. It's the kind of work that many of us are afraid of doing because it involves looking inside our own hearts and souls and beginning to heal the wounds that have been there for a long time.

But, I hope, dear reader, that sharing my journey will inspire you that this is work worth doing. I hope I can inspire you to look inside, dig deep, and find that vast well of love within. The greatest treasures are buried deep under the ocean, and the greatest source of love is from the endless supply we already have inside ourselves. For if we can find love within ourselves, it will pour out into love for each other. And if we can find love for each other, then we will be able to find love for all the living things on the planet.

\* \* \*

My journey to finding that love began sixteen years ago when I found the practices of yoga[4], but the yearning for it began even earlier than that.

I have worn many hats in my life. I'm a practicing architect, designing commercial buildings for the last twenty years. I always thought of myself as a problem solver and a planner, though am now learning to let go of that need to plan and problem solve everything. In addition to the role of Architect, I call myself a wife, a stepmother, a runner, a yoga teacher, a shamanic healer, an earth keeper, and a writer. The biggest constant, through all those roles, was a persistent yearning in my soul to go deeper - deeper in my thoughts, reflections, and actions. I have always been the one to dig deep, to try and understand the bigger picture, and to ask the big questions.

I am also a dreamer. Since I can remember I have always had big dreams, both sleeping and awake. Dreams that I didn't always understand, but I knew were important. Sometimes those dreams turned into poems, short stories, or informed my designs. Sometimes they gave me clues as to what I needed to fix in my life. Often they just stayed quiet in my heart, as I hadn't learned the language of how to express them.

I love to be in nature. I've always loved walking in the woods or swimming in the ocean. Maybe that love is what drew me to shamanism, and to reconnect with the Earth on a deeper level. My happiest days are when I am hiking or running in the mountains of the beautiful state of Colorado which I call home. And on my saddest days, nature can be my best companion. No matter what is going on in life, I can always find peace when I spend just a short time in nature.

---

[4] **YOGA:** When referencing Yoga I am referring to the broader spiritual and holistic approach or lifestyle. The word Yoga in Sanskrit means *"to unite"* or *"to connect"*. The practices of yoga, be they asana, breath-work, or meditation, are intended to bring us into connection with the bigger universal consciousness.

Being someone who always wanted to go deeper, dream big, feel big feelings, and question everything made life challenging sometimes. When I was young, I felt like I was on a constant roller coaster, and didn't know how to navigate those highs and lows. Sixteen years ago, I found yoga to help me balance those emotional ups and downs. Fate brought me to a yoga tradition that was based on ancient tantric teachings, and was much more than the physical asana[5] practices of most American-style yoga. Yoga became an important part of my personal and spiritual life; it helped me to find balance and to develop an independent 'witness' of my own life. Yoga helped me weather the many storms that came my way raising step-children and building my career. But it wasn't until my own life crisis that it really came to the forefront.

Two years ago, my healthy, energetic mother was diagnosed with an aggressive cancer, and nine months later she was gone. This devastating loss pushed me to re-examine all that was important to me. I found great comfort in my yoga practices, especially the relaxation practice of yoga nidra[6], but I needed something more.

I recalled a shamanic healing I had received a few years prior. I had even saved the little paper where she had read in my oracle cards that one day I would be a light worker! Also written on that paper was the

---

5 **ASANA: (Aw-SA-Naw)**A Sanskrit word that means 'sitting down', it is generally used to talk about various postures in yoga. The end goal of these postures is to provide balance in the body as well as flexibility so that one can comfortably 'sit down' and practice meditation with ease.

6 **YOGA NIDRA (Yoga Nee-dra):** The translation of this practice means 'yogic sleep'. This is a relaxation practice that is based on ancient yoga teachings to allow ourselves to withdraw our senses from the external world and come to the internal world. It is a systematic 'letting go' of the external senses, the body, and the breath and finally coming to a place of internal relaxation. It puts the practitioner into a brainwave state between awake and asleep and is a practice that can assist with meditation.

name of the institute she had learned from, The Four Winds. That slip of paper brought me to the teachings of shamanism[7].

Over the next several months, I experienced what I can only describe as an awakening. While at my mother's home, cleaning out her things, I had several powerful shamanic meditations. They showed me that I had to make a change and that the time was now. They called me to step into the unknown and embark on a journey where I did not know the destination. They called me to choose my heart's path over safety and status quo, and to begin to walk a new path to love and light.

Shamanism and yoga helped me through my darkest days of grief, healing me in ways that I didn't even know were possible. As I have come into unconditional love for myself and others, I have shed many stories from my life. I have shed the stories of not being enough, the

---

[7] **SHAMANISM**: The word Shaman is Siberian in origin and was a person that acted on behalf of their community or tribe as an intermediary between the spirit world, the natural world, and the tribe. They were someone who was in touch with the unseen and the seen realms. The word shaman and shamanism are becoming universally adopted words that refer to the spiritual and traditional practices of native cultures around the world and the practitioners who share those teachings.So many countries have different words for these practices. Shaman is a word that is being used in the English language to help create a bridge between those traditions. Though they are all different, they all have a few common themes. First, they respect nature and all living things, acknowledging that humans are a part of the natural order, not above or superior to it. Second, they respect the ancestors and the wisdom they share. Third, they acknowledge there is both a seen and unseen world. This unseen world could be called magic, but with the advancement of physics and science, it is now also understood as the energy that connects all things.

stories of the patriarchy[8] and colonialism[9] of Western Society, and their stories of fear and scarcity. I embraced the teachings of love, balance, and harmony with each other and the planet. I am working to live in Ayni, where humans live in a reciprocal relationship with each other and all living things.

This book offers practices and teachings from both yoga and shamanism. The yoga teachings are from the lineage of Swami Satyananda and the Bihar School of Yoga[10]. The books and teachings of this lineage go deep into the ancient yogic texts, the understanding of neuroscience and anatomy, and the workings of the mind and the energy body. Through disciplined practices or 'sadhanas'[11], they provide a roadmap

---

[8] **PATRIARCHY**: Patriarchy is a system of government in which men hold the power and largely exclude women from participation in that government. This book acknowledges that for at least the last 2000 years this has been the predominant method of government in Western culture and that women and feminine qualities have been considered inferior, lesser, and undesirable in our society.

[9] **COLONIALISM**: Colonialism is the practice of one country taking full or partial control over another country or culture. In this book specifically, I reference the idea of colonialism as it relates to white Europeans and their systematic conquering and exploitation of black, indigenous and people of color around the world, especially in the Americas. Colonialism is closely tied to the concept of 'Manifest Destiny' where Europeans felt it was their divine right to steal lands from native peoples and take them for their own.

[10] **SWAMI**: A Swami is the name given to a Hindu religious teacher, and is used as a title for a person with authority. It means "He who is one with himself". Swamiji is used as a stand-in for a person's name and in this book references the Swamis I have learned directly from in my yoga teachings.

[11] **SADHANA: (Saw-Da-Na)** A Sanskrit word that means realization or achievement. It refers to a daily and disciplined spiritual practice. The goal of this practice is to subdue the ego and eventually transcend the self. It often refers to a group of practices that can be a roadmap to enlightenment, such as practicing asana (postures), pranayama (breathing practices), and meditation on a daily basis.

to developing our higher wisdom and our independent observer or 'witness'.

The shamanic teachings are from the Four Winds Medicine Wheel as developed by Alberto Villoldo, Ph.D., and my experiences doing the energy medicine training with the Four Winds Institute. The Four Winds teaches shamanism based on the teachings of the Q'ero Shamans of Peru. It combines ancient wisdom and traditions with modern neuroscience. It acknowledges that beyond our physical body, we have a luminous energy field that surrounds each of us. That field contains the blueprint for our entire existence as well as our connection to and with the Universe. In life, traumas, negative stories, or other imprints appear on the field and must be cleared to help us come back into right relationship with ourselves and the Universe.

I hope these different teachings can be complementary and not confusing. I come from a basic belief that Yoga, Shamanism, Buddhism, the Abrahamic religions of Judaism, Christianity and Islam, and other spiritual modalities are not exclusive practices. They all have things to teach and wisdom to offer. And so, I share these ideas freely with you, regardless of your spiritual or cultural background. Each of us has our own unique connection with the Divine, and I hope the teachings in this book can be considered universal, even if the terminologies and practices have their own flavor.

I had a yoga teacher long ago that broke down the different teachings of Hinduism, Buddhism, Islam, and Christianity. She explained how they were all similar at their core, but rooted in different cultural expressions. Each Holy person in these lineages taught that spirituality should be rooted in the ideas of love, compassion, and forming a relationship with the Divine. Finding your path is about finding the one that speaks to your heart. In my path, the teachings of yoga and shamanism spoke to my heart and have helped me grow love and compassion. They have informed my own relationship with the divine aspects of the Universe.

As I have gone deeply into these practices of shamanism and yoga, I find the language and techniques vary, but the fundamental beliefs are the same. The ancient sages and mystics knew and understood the mind-body-spirit connection in a much more profound way than we do now, and so we look to their ancient wisdom to uncover these long-forgotten secrets.

I believe that we are our own best teachers, but the world also offers wisdom and teachers to help us along the way. If any of these practices spark an interest in you to go deeper, I would encourage you to look into deeper training or finding teachers to help you on your path. The practices in this book are not a substitute for an authentic teaching experience but can still be used extensively for your own inner reflections. I acknowledge I come from a Western colonial background and am still a novice in these practices that have been passed down for millennia. While I have spent years studying them, I do not pretend to be an "expert" on anything other than my own life and my own experiences.

So now that we're all on the same page, let's get started!

\* \* \*

# AYNI

\* \* \*

# 3

# Looking Back, Looking Forward

*"Not till we are completely lost or turned around... do we begin to find ourselves"*
*—Henry David Thoreau*

When I was a kid, I was a deep thinker. It certainly didn't make me the most popular kid in school, but I couldn't help it. I was always the one that asked why. I was the one that wanted to volunteer the answer because I was genuinely interested in what we were learning. I loved math, writing, reading, art, music, and science. I loved learning. All of it. I also loved being in nature, twirling around, or sitting in the grass making clover necklaces. I loved walking through the woods singing songs and swimming at the beach trying to hear the dolphins under the waves. I was full of joy, love, and curiosity.

Truthfully, it was people I didn't understand. I didn't understand why they would tease and hurt someone and think it was funny, or why they would withhold love to gain favor. I didn't understand why they would hide their light from the world and tell others to do so as well. Yes, most people thought I was a weird kid.

But I didn't realize I was weird until others told me so. They told me to stop raising my hand all the time and that I needed to walk in a straight line at school. They told me that my clothes should match, that plaid and stripes were NOT a good combination. That I was not good at athletics, so I should stop trying. They told me that it was okay to be smart, but not 'too' smart. That women should be quiet and controlled, but it was okay for boys to be unruly and outspoken. They told me my looks were for others to judge, not myself, and that I was chubby, awkward, and didn't fit in.

I believed it all and more. As do we all. We all believe these stories that we are told when we are young. They are the framework by which we find our place in the world. The first 20 years shape our view of ourselves and the world. And then maybe we will spend the next 20 years undoing it all! Re-discovering who we really are and coming back to the love and joy that we had right there in the beginning.

Since I didn't always know what to do with my body or feelings, I worked on developing my mind. I felt my body was an awkward thing to be ashamed of, and I kept my emotions in a nice, neat, little ball, because expressing them rarely worked out for me. I decided to become an architect where I could use my mind to solve problems. It was the perfect blend for the girl who was both creative and good at math. As an architect, I could listen to people's needs and wants and then transform them into a building. I listened, planned, and acted. The measure of my worth was in what actions I took, what problems I solved, and what external validations I received in doing so. I did quite well with this for many years. But, like so many, I was still caught up in the whirlwind of stress, anxiety, worry, low self-esteem, declining health, and all the other problems that are benchmarks of our society.

And, as you can guess, my emotions didn't stay in a neat, little ball. They would come out in extremes - happiness, sadness, and anger. While everything appeared great on the surface, in truth I was lost, out of balance, and always looking for love and happiness. And of course,

I was always looking for that OUTSIDE of me, not inside. I had lost that little girl who was already full of joy, love, and wonder. She had been silenced by years of conformity.

But she would not be silenced entirely. She would question still. In my unhappiness, she would ask, *"Why? Why are you unhappy? What can you do to change? We can't settle for this!"*

In the first decade of my professional career, I worked at five different architectural firms, always hoping to find happiness in the next job. It wasn't until I started going deeper into myself that I realized that elusive happiness could only be found within me. Yes, I had a loving husband and two beautiful step-sons, but their love could not bring me true happiness. Yes, I had a successful job and a great house, but that could not bring me happiness either. Only as I found love for myself did I begin to find true happiness.

And finding love for ourselves, real love, is harder than it sounds! There is a lot of social conditioning that has been put in our way. There are a lot of stories—that we aren't good enough, pretty enough, smart enough, rich enough, strong enough—that keep us from coming into a good relationship with ourselves. These stories are part of the colonial and patriarchal mindset. They come from a basic premise that humanity is flawed and imperfect, that we are cut off from the love and light of the Universe. They come from a mindset that wants to keep people in their place so they don't shine too brightly, lest someone else's power be threatened. However, the indigenous and shamanic teachings do not agree with this mindset. They say that we have all the love and light of the Universe within us; we just need to reconnect with it.

Across the world, we are seeing a renewed interest in indigenous practices and ways of life. I call them shamanism, but there are many words for them. These philosophies are Earth-based and deeply rooted in the feminine aspects of creativity and nurturing. They are based on the idea that the Divine is within us and that we can connect with the universal Divine consciousness. "God" is not sitting on a cloud throne somewhere far removed from all creation, but is within us and part of us.

I believe this renewed interest is a natural awakening and is coming at a critical time in our history. Just as I am trying to unlearn the stories people told me as a child and come back to that girl full of love and wonder, so are many others. Women are in search of their own Divine Feminine as they throw off the ideas that women are less, or that the qualities of nurturing and compassion are somehow 'inferior' qualities to power and strength. Men are in search of healing their own Divine Masculine, acknowledging that power has been misused and that many examples of masculinity in our society are toxic ones. And many people are exploring their gender expression and their unique relationship to both the masculine and feminine aspects. We no longer accept that an assigned gender must dictate our behaviors, feelings, or expressions.

I do not think any of this is a coincidence. It is all part of a bigger turning over of the world where we are beginning to uncover the secrets long covered. The power dynamic is shifting, and the idea that the answers to life are only to be found outside of us is cracking open. We are starting to believe we can find the answers within us, that we can find it in community, and in sharing. But we have been so long in isolation we are struggling to know how. We have forgotten how to listen to ourselves, and so we are afraid of the unknown.

But don't be afraid my friend, be brave! Be brave to go on this journey to self-discovery to find love and happiness within. What I used to see as problems and traumas, I now see as opportunities to grow and find more love. Fear can be a gift to show us a path to healing. And the darkness is only scary until we turn the light on.

Also know, we are not alone in this great shift. There is a whole community out there ready to support us on our journey. Our fellow humans, the plants, the animals, the wind, the water, we are all on this planet together, and we are all trying to find love, balance, and harmony.

\* \* \*

# AYNI

***

# 4

# Falling in love with "Me"

*"Knowing yourself is the beginning of all wisdom"*
   *-Aristotle*

So, what do you think of when you say the word "me?" You probably think about your body for sure: your bones, organs, lungs, and heart. You may think about your mind, your emotions, or maybe your idea of a soul. These are all parts of us, and it's important to remember that. No one part is more important than the other. Each one interacts with the other—science has shown that they are interconnected.

If the body is in pain, it can cause emotional or mental pain. If the mind or emotions are in disharmony, then they can manifest in physical pain and illnesses. Heart disease, cancers, and auto-immune disorders have all been shown to have mental and emotional components. Stress and anxiety have huge impacts on our bodies and can cause migraines, chronic pain, and other disorders.

The ancient texts of yoga teach that our "body" is made of different sheaths or koshas, a bit like an onion. Each kosha is part of our overall body and they are all connected. They go from the gross to the subtle and are:

# The Koshas or 'Sheaths' of the Body

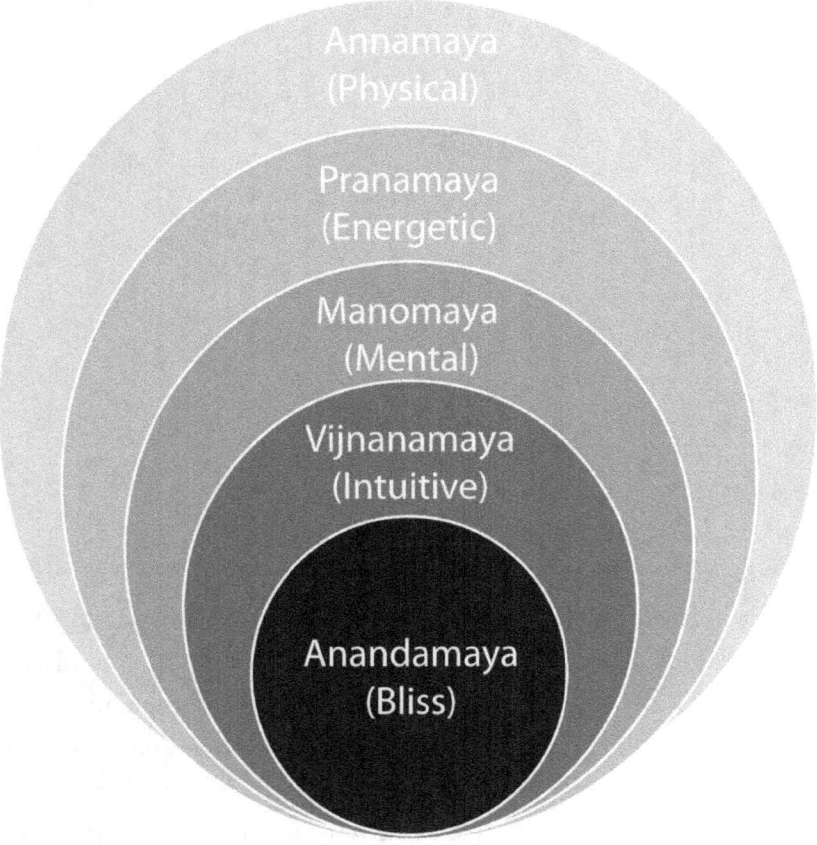

- Annamaya-kosha (the physical or food sheath)
- Pranamaya-kosha (the energy sheath)
- Manomaya-kosha (the mental sheath)
- Vijnanamaya-kosha (the intellect/intuitive sheath)
- Anandamaya-kosha (the bliss sheath)

The Shamanic teachings from the Four Winds also talk about the body on these different levels, from physical to emotional, spiritual to energetic. In this lineage, they are represented by archetypes, animal symbols that can be used as mythical guides, as well as being associated with cardinal directions.

Together they create the Four Winds medicine wheel, and by journeying through that wheel one can find complete and holistic healing. These four archetypes are:

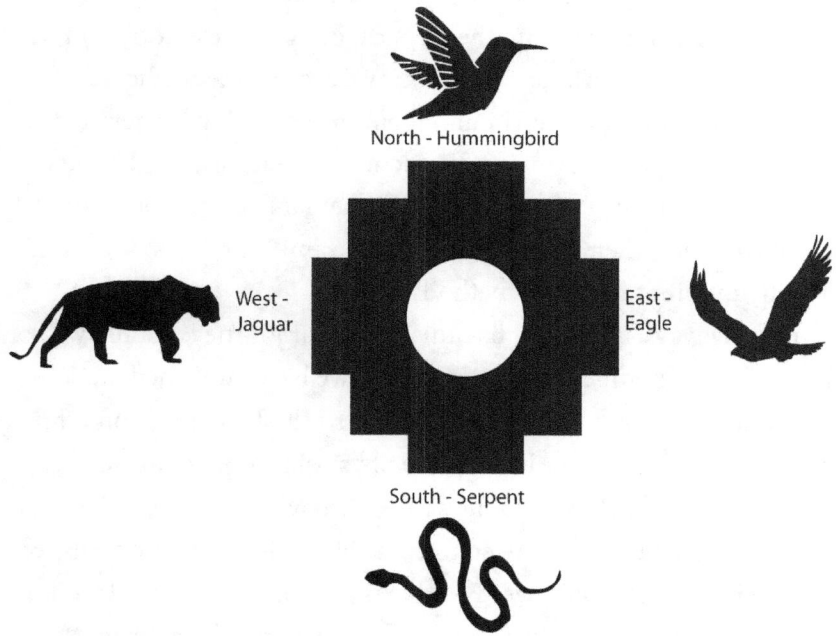

North - Hummingbird

West - Jaguar

East - Eagle

South - Serpent

- Serpent – The physical aspect, Direction of South
- Jaguar – The emotional aspect, Direction of West
- Hummingbird – The Spiritual Aspect, Direction of North
- Eagle – The Energetic Aspect where all is interconnected, Direction

of East

Both of these traditions agree that we should work on the physical aspect before we move on to the emotional, spiritual, or energetic aspects. To be balanced, we should start from the "gross" and move to the "subtle" in our healing. If you spend a lot of time developing your spiritual aspect but haven't balanced the body or the emotions, then they will always drag you back down to their level. I found this to be true in my own life, and it's how I will shape this book.

The book will move from the physical body to the emotional body to the soul/energetic body. We will travel around the medicine wheel from Serpent to Jaguar to Hummingbird to Eagle. I will reference the shamanic and yoga teaching and practices for each aspect. I hope you will see that the teachings of yoga and shamanism are closely linked, as I have found them to be. They tell the same story even if they use slightly different words or methods.

In many ways, it will feel like this is a linear journey, but life works in a circle. Sometimes as soon as we feel we have awakened ourselves up to love and light and feel connected to the Universe, something comes around to take us back to the physical level. We can get a cold or injury and forget everything we just discovered. Or we will have a devastating life event and need to come back to our emotional aspect to provide healing and love. But this is part of the process, too. Life and healing move in circles, but with every turn of the wheel, those circles can become more balanced and harmonious. When we begin to find balance in all of these aspects of ourselves, we can move back and forth between them with more ease. The challenges of life will rock us but not knock us completely over. I like to think of it like a ship in the ocean. There will always be waves, but when we are in a place of balance and harmony, the waves are less likely to capsize the ship. We have a better captain, a better crew, and a better boat to navigate the waves of life.

\* \* \*

Many years ago when I found yoga, I was looking for a way to de-stress and to help with my roller coaster of emotions. I thought it would help promote my mind-body connection, to allow me to relax. It did all that and more. It started my long, slow journey to self-love and body acceptance. I traveled around the U.S., Canada, and even India to learn from Swamis and Gurus. Yoga taught me to develop my "witness" or independent observer to my thoughts, feelings, and emotions. It taught me that I am more than my thoughts and "monkey mind," and more than my feelings and emotions. If I can witness these, from a higher perspective, I can begin to see myself and my struggles in a more objective way.

Slowly, very slowly, I began to see myself from that witness, developing self-love and also questioning some of the stories I had been telling myself. But I didn't begin to scratch the surface of all the toxic stories I had developed until I finally started running.

I was what most people would have called a chubby kid. It wasn't that I didn't like being outside or playing, but from an early age I heard the story loud and clear that I was not athletic and not very coordinated. I was always picked last at gym class, and team sports didn't work out well for me. So like a self-fulfilling prophecy, I retreated away from physical activity. I loved playing soccer with my best friend but I could never play on a team, because I wasn't fast enough or coordinated enough. I excelled at academics, so I put my energy into that. I graduated high school early, went to a prestigious university, and flourished in my career as an architect. I lived in my mind almost exclusively. My body was just an annoyance, the cause of my low self-esteem. My heart was also a liability, as it was entirely too sensitive and passionate. I felt only my mind could be relied upon. But as the years passed, my stories, like all false stories, began to unravel. For there is more than one aspect of us, and living in any one of them for your entire life will not a balanced human make.

As I raised two boys, I realized we all have different things we are good at or struggle with. One of my stepsons struggled with academics but excelled in all the physical things that I was challenged with. The other did well in academics and sports but seemed to struggle sharing his feelings. As I share my story, I invite you to think about what aspects resonate with you in your own life. What part of you did you tell yourself you were "no good at?" What part of you have you shut down or disowned? Do you miss the idea of having it in your life? Do you ever feel a yearning for the time when you didn't think it was broken or less than?

Now ask yourself, why did you shut it down? Is it because someone told you that you weren't good enough? That you weren't smart enough? Or pretty enough or fast enough? Did someone tell you that your writing was so-so or that your painting was just average? Did someone tell you that you certainly won't be on the volleyball team with that mediocre serve?

Now, ask yourself, who cares? Really....who cares? I am never going to be an Olympic athlete, but does that mean that I should shut down my relationship with my body for the rest of my life? I will probably not become a world-famous architect, but does that mean that I should not be one at all?

Each of us has our own stories of inadequacy to examine on our own path to self-love. No matter what they are, the idea is the same—look at them and ask yourself if they are serving you or hurting you. Ask if these are truths or if they are self-judgments we made a long time ago. To find balance and harmony in ourselves, we need to find out where the imbalance is so that we can begin to heal that part of us. We need to heal it so that we can become a complete and whole person. We can finally become the full "me."

For me, I found balance and harmony in my body through running. I had always loved the idea of running. I would even have dreams about it. In my dreams, I would bound down a mountainside like I was almost flying. I imagined what it would feel like to feel the rhythm of my feet moving in a graceful dance, one-two, one-two. There was such freedom in the idea of running for me. But when I tried running as a kid, my face would turn beet red, I would be out of breath, and the other kids would leave me in their dust. I tried again and again, but it was always just too hard. So it stayed a dream.

As I grew older, I gained weight and became less active until even hiking was a challenge. I had a poor relationship with food, looking at it as a comfort source, not a fuel source. I had a poor relationship with my body, looking at it with disdain and sometimes disgust, like it was external from me. It was like I was my mind, and my body was just the problem from which my low self-esteem had grown. I thought I was working on a mind-body-spirit connection in my yoga, acknowledging the importance of stretching and breathing, but it was like my body was still on the sidelines, watching from afar, being judged and shamed.

But thankfully the Universe knew better than to let me continue in my downward spiral. I had a co-worker who was an avid runner. At the time, we were working on a project together and would spend many hours in the car each week. I would pick his brain as to why he would run 10, 20, and 30 miles in a day. He told me how he just loved movement, loved being in nature, and seeing all the things he could see in a day. He loved pushing himself, to see where his limits were. He felt running was a big stress release, where he could just be in the present and not think about anything else. This sounded great! These talks rekindled my dream. As he talked about being in nature, the peace he found in movement, and the feeling of satisfaction after a good long run, it lit a spark inside me that had been long asleep.

I shared my insecurities as to how I couldn't run, how I was slow and out of shape, but he didn't shut me down the way the kids had. He was encouraging and made me feel like maybe I could do it. I started running on the treadmill, but then my face would get beet red, I would get out of breath, and all the stories from my childhood came back. So, I gave up, again. I was just too heavy to do this, I told myself. Even people I talked to would tell me to give up. They suggested I should lose weight first and then run, otherwise it was bad for my knees. But I felt the only way I could become more active was to lose weight and the only way to lose weight was to become more active, and I couldn't do either. There was just something WRONG with me.

It was right around this time that I was on a beach vacation with my husband and, on a whim, we decided to sign up for a shamanic energy healing session. I was curious and wondered if they could figure out why my legs hurt. For the last year, I had a mysterious tightness in my calves. No amount of stretching would fix it, and there was no medical explanation. It felt like ropes were tied around my legs, always weighing me down. The shaman did not magically erase the pain that day, but her work did create a shift, and I think that shift began the dominoes that changed my life.

Do you believe in coincidence? I do not. I believe in synchronicity. I believe when something comes up out of the blue, as if coincidence, it's not a coincidence at all. It is the Universe trying to help you on your path. Weeks after that shamanic energy healing, I chanced upon a book that gave me the courage to finally change my life.

It was a free Amazon Prime read called, *A Beautiful Work in Progress* by Mirna Valerio. Mirna is a self-described fat girl who runs ultra-marathons (distances longer than 26 miles). She is also Black, running in a very White-dominated sport. She is a trailblazer in so many ways, and her book changed my life. Here was a fat girl, like me, overcoming all sorts of obstacles, much greater than my own. And she did it with a smile on her face and love for herself. She was courageous and brave and also kind to herself and her body as she pushed it to see how far it wanted to go. She acknowledged her fears and did things anyway. She wasn't running "to lose weight," she was running because she loved it. She may lose weight or not lose weight, because whatever weight she was, she was still "Enough", just as she was.

*"Wow!"* I thought to myself. What a concept.

And so, with her book as encouragement, I tried once again. I signed up for a 5k race, so I couldn't back out, and started running. I used an app called the Couch to 5k program and did interval running (running with walking breaks) until I got to the point where I could run 5k or 3.1 miles without stopping. When I complained about my body soreness, my husband listened but encouraged me to move through it. It was hard. My face would turn beet red, I was out of breath, and everything was sore. I had to ice my knees a lot that first month. I learned all new stretches for my legs so my knees would stop hurting. But I kept digging deep, because I knew somewhere deep down, that this was more than just me running a 5k. This was me un-telling myself all those stories that I was a failure, that I couldn't do it, that I was weak. This was me finding strength, power, and love in my body. And guess what—I did it! I ran a 5k! At 38 years old I had become a runner, and I loved it!

I loved the feeling of strength and power in my basic physical existence.

It was so new to me, as I'd spent most of my life in my mind. My knees finally stopped hurting, and that mysterious pain in my calves went away. Completely! And it's never come back. I loved this feeling so much, and I wanted to see how much more I was capable of. I ran a 10k, and another, and then I trained to run a half marathon (13.1 miles). I dedicated each mile of that half marathon to the people who had encouraged me and to the people that had shut me down. Without both of them, I would not have been where I was that day. I was slow, to be sure. I still had to take walk breaks, but it didn't matter. I was running. I was moving my body, and I was loving my body.

In my enthusiasm for movement, I encouraged my sister and father to start running, and we all ran a race together. We ran over the Annapolis Bay Bridge, six miles over the beautiful Chesapeake Bay in Maryland. It was a special day for all of us. I grew up in Annapolis, and when my sister and I were little our dad ran that race. To come full circle and all run it together was a defining moment in my life.

Then, after about a year of running, I decided to train for a marathon. That's 26.2 miles! I picked a training plan that included lots of slow miles to help build up endurance for the big day. I think it topped off at 55 miles in one week. For me, that was about 12 hours of running in one week! Everything I read about marathon training talked about how important it was to adequately fuel our bodies. And at 55 miles in a week, my body needed some premium fuel. I began to think of my body as a race car, needing premium fuel for premium performance. I started listening to what it asked for. What was the premium fuel it wanted? Was it carbs or protein? Sugar or fats? Vegetables? What did it crave? It asked for spinach, lots of spinach, so I gave it spinach. It asked for quality protein, for vegetables, and to drink less alcohol. I gave it all these things, and it gave me a marathon. It gave me 26.2 miles of moving my body. And so finally, at 40 years old, I began to have a healthy and balanced relationship with my body.

My journey was from a place of non-movement to a place of embracing movement. It was coming back into a balanced and loving relationship with my body. I understand that there are many of us out there that are quite sedentary and that there are also many of us out there that are addicted to movement. Both of these are out of balance if taken to extremes.

In yoga, they teach we all have three qualities of our being, or gunas. Guna is a Sanskrit word that means a quality or tendency. These teachings say we exhibit all three of these gunas in ourselves, and the amount of each changes throughout life. The first is tamas, which means inertia. It is a sluggish and low energy quality. If someone is very tamasic they can feel stuck, tired, and not able to move forward. They may feel depressed and apathetic. The second is rajas, which means energy and movement. It is the opposite of tamas. If someone is in a rajasic state they might have trouble sitting still and are always on the move. They may be quick to anger, or feel anxious. The last is sattva, which is balance. This is a state of balance and harmony, where the qualities of tamas and rajas are reduced and a person feels joy, peace, and contentment. When a person is in sattva they are able to access that higher version of themselves.

If we are too much in tamas or rajas, we are not in balance. Only by incorporating both inertia and movement, can we come into real balance. For some of us, our bodies are asking for movement. For others, it is asking for rest. To find balance, first we need to listen.

Is your body asking for better nourishment or to bring more stretching into your life? Is it asking for you to reduce your stress and practice mindfulness? Whatever it may be asking for, the first thing we have to do is ask. Then we have to listen, really listen to our body's wants and needs. My body's big ask was to run, to be a runner, to dance over the rocks on a trail in the mountains. It was to break down the self-defeating stories of my childhood that I was weak and awkward and embrace movement and strength. It was to find love and acceptance in what my body did and not just what it looked like.

For someone else, your body might be craving for you to look at it in the mirror with love and acceptance. For someone else, your body may be asking for you to take up rock climbing! Whatever your body's deepest desire is, know that it's a call to come to a place of self-love, balance, and acceptance.

\* \* \*

## Practice: Listening to Our Body

Here is an exercise you can try at home to find awareness and begin to listen to your body. Know that all the answers you seek are already right there inside you, all we have to do is listen.

Find somewhere where you won't be disturbed for 5-10 minutes. Then lay down on the bed or the floor or sit comfortably in a chair with your legs in a comfortable, relaxed position, your spine straight, and arms to your sides or resting on your thighs. Close your eyes and take three deep breaths in, exhaling fully with each breath. Next, we will begin a full scan of the body. Bring an idea of an independent observer, someone outside of you, looking at your body without judgment or opinion. Now take that observer mindset and start to look at each part of the body. Say it, visualize it, feel it with a detached witness. Start with the right side. Bring attention to each finger on the right hand, the hand itself, the right wrist, the right arm, and the shoulder. Do you notice any discomfort? Tingling? Messages? If so, notice them with curiosity and awareness, not judgment. Move on to the right side of the chest, waist, hip, right thigh, knee, low leg, ankle, and right foot. Notice each toe on the right foot. Again, just notice the body. If there is something that calls to your attention, notice it, but don't overanalyze.

Move now to the left side of the body. Scan the fingers on the left hand, the hand itself, left wrist, arm, elbow, shoulder, the left side of the chest, waist, hip, thigh, knee, low leg, ankle, and left foot. Scan each toe of the left foot. Notice anything that calls for attention. Now, scan the head, the forehead, the eyes, the ears, the nose, the jaw, and the neck. Check in with the front of your body, the heart space. Feel into the stomach, the organs surrounding your stomach. Feel the hips and pelvis area. Check in with the back side of the body; feeling the back of the legs, the buttocks, the low back, middle back, upper back, and the shoulder blades. Then just check in with the whole body. Feel your entire body, in all its interconnectedness. Feel the legs and their joints. Feel the arms and their joints, feel the whole body. Now give yourself a moment to reflect on the miracle that is your body; all these parts working together to allow movement and life.

Now take a few deep breaths and come back to full awareness of your surroundings. Make a few movements, stretching the legs and arms, ensuring you've come back to an awake state. Did anything speak to you? If so, write that down. Write down what hurt and what felt peaceful. Write down if anything asked you for help. Write down if anything felt out of balance. Try to do this without judgment. Now ask yourself, is anything needed to come back into balance and harmony in the body? Did anything bring up feelings of disharmony or pain? Are there any actions you can take to help bring love to that part? That action may be one of movement or changing a habit, or it may be one of self-acceptance, just coming to the understanding that you are ENOUGH, as you are right now.

Space For Journaling - What messages did you get from this body scan practice?

*\* \* \**

The trees do not look at other trees and worry about if one is taller than the other or broader or narrower. They understand that the sun, the rain, and the soil all had an influence to create them as they are today, twists and turns and all. Those that might look gnarly overcame great hardship to even exist, and their twisted trunk is a testament to their resilience. The tree knows inherently that while its current shape was influenced by the past, the future is still to be determined. I invite you all to become trees, to shed our feelings of self-judgment, and embrace our bodies with self-love and full acceptance.

*\* \* \**

# 5

# Intro to Shamanism

*"In the universe, there are things that are known, and things that are unknown, and in between, there are doors."*
– William Blake

## The Way of the Serpent

In my shamanic training at the Four Winds Institute, the physical aspect is represented by the archetype symbol of the Serpent. Historically, the serpent has many meanings. In Hinduism, it is the Kundalini, our life force. In Christianity, it tempted Eve to get the knowledge of good and evil by tasting from the Tree of Life. In Western medicine, we see two serpents coming together on a staff as a symbol of healing. In shamanism, the serpent offers the wisdom of the Earth, her belly close to the ground and in tune with nature.

The Teaching of the Serpent has four fundamental lessons. The teachings are:

- Non-Suffering
- Non-Judgment
- Non-Attachment
- Beauty

As we look at our bodies, our lives, and our physical existence, do we embody these teachings? Do we practice non-judgment with ourselves and others? Do we see beauty in ourselves?

Take a moment and think about how you look at yourself and others on this physical level. Do you practice all these teachings? If you answer no, that's okay! It's just being truthful with yourself. And being truthful and authentic is Step One to coming into a good relationship with ourselves.

* * *

## Non-Suffering

Non-Suffering means exactly what it says—stop suffering! Life does not have to be endless suffering, and yet somehow it's all we as humans come back to. Some might say humanity is addicted to suffering. Non-suffering means that even if painful things happen, we do not have to write great, big stories about them. Things can just happen, and then we can move on.

We are very good at taking a set of "facts" and writing all sorts of stories about them. I wrote a story that I could not run based on the fact that I would get red in the face when I ran as a child. This story then grew into a bigger story that I was physically weak and deficient, and it shaped my life. These stories get so big, we believe they are facts, and we suffer because of them. We base our lives on fabricated stories and can then miss out on our complete and authentic selves.

The Buddhists, Yogis, and Shamans all agree that suffering is caused when our inner perspective, our inner world, is out of alignment with the reality that we perceive. Our ability to change our reality is limited, though many do try. It's much easier, and takes much less energy, to instead change our perspective. Changing our perspective can help us on this path to non-suffering.

My yoga Swami gave a wonderful example of this. We may go to the mall to look for a certain outfit to wear to a special event. Maybe it's an event that we've been waiting for all year. We have in our mind exactly what we want—the color, the cut, how it looks on us. In our mind it's perfect. We go to the mall, but we do not find that outfit. We try things on, we go from store to store, but nothing looks like it did in our mind. We try another mall and still cannot find that outfit. And so we suffer. We may suddenly not even want to go to the event, because how can we go without that perfect outfit?

Our excitement turns to despair, and we are faced with two choices. We can change reality so that it can meet our expectations. We could keep shopping at more stores, ordering outfits online, have the outfit custom made, and spend many more hours and energy to create the perfect outfit that currently doesn't exist. Or we can change our perspective. We can realign ourselves with the reality of the world around us. The reality is that this outfit doesn't exist the way we saw it in our mind. That is the fact. So what story will we dream up about it?

If we are trapped in the world of suffering, we will dream up a story that the world is against us, or a story of self-judgment. We may blame the fashion industry, or blame ourselves for not looking the way we want to. But, if we can be open to the world as it is, rather than what we want it to be, the story can be quite different.

Maybe we will go back to the first store and find an outfit that is indeed flattering, especially when we accept our figure as it is. Or we could find that an outfit we already had, dressed up with accessories, is actually a perfect outfit. Maybe we would remember the event is for people we love who honestly don't care about what we wear in the first place. It is our perspective that often dictates whether the world is full of abundance and joy or scarcity and fear. It is our perspective that will decide if we live in a place of suffering or non-suffering.

* * *

## Non-Judgment

Non-judgment means we work to get rid of these stories lovingly and compassionately. We do not judge ourselves because we have these stories, but we must begin to discern truth from fiction. This is how we free ourselves from these false stories and come back to our authentic selves.

When you reflect on yourself, look at the ideas you have held as truths. Look at the morals that you hold, and where they came from. How do we practice discernment in looking at ourselves? We must remove the idea of judgment from our thoughts and reflections. Discernment means to see things as neither good nor bad, but just as they are at that moment.

Ask yourself, what story do I have that is preventing me from coming into harmony with myself? What story is holding me back? As we practice discernment and non-judgment, we can examine our stories and begin to unravel those that are hurting us more than helping us. We can begin to shed these stories, like the serpent sheds its skin, and write new stories of joy and abundance.

But this takes some work. We are so good at judging! Judging ourselves and each other. How do we perceive ourselves without judgment? How do we discern which stories are hurting us and need to be shed? We must develop our non-judging selves.

Our inner judge is the loudest voice we often hear. Comparatively, the non-judging self is so quiet it's practically a whisper. We can also call these two sides of ourselves the Ego and the Intuition. We could call them the big annoying voice in our head and the small quiet voice. In my yoga practices, we would call them the monkey mind and the higher mind or witness. It doesn't matter the words we use. What matters is this—if we only listen to the Ego, we will always stay in a place of fear and scarcity. We will never be able to shed our stories and come to a world full of joy and abundance.

We must learn to differentiate between our Ego and our Intuition.

\* \* \*

## Practice: Differentiate Between Ego and Intuition

Begin to identify your Ego's voice and your Intuition's voice. Next time you hear a voice in your head, ask if that is your Ego speaking or your Intuition. Ask yourself four questions.

1. Is that voice talking to you lovingly or from a place of fear or anger?
2. Is that voice giving you a laundry list of reasons you can't do something or is it short and sweet in its message?
3. Is it talking to you from a place of scarcity, that there won't be enough of something? Or is it talking to you from a place of confidence?

4. Is it calm and compassionate? Or is it acting judgmental and controlling?

Write down the answers you hear about that voice.

Here are some characteristics of ego vs. intuition.

Ego: Speaks loudly. This voice usually comes from the mind or heart in the body rather than the gut. You may feel tightness in those places when it speaks. It talks from a place of fear and scarcity. It rambles, it changes its mind, and it gives you a laundry list of reasons you can't do something.

Intuition: It is quiet, calm, and steadfast. It usually speaks from the gut. It does not create feelings of tension in the body. It does not change its message, and it speaks from a place of love. It is encouraging.

Yoga offers practices that are very helpful in developing the Intuition, or witness. The practice in the previous chapter of doing the body scan is one such practice and is called yoga nidra. There are many others—breathing practices, asana, meditations—they can all help us develop our witness and quiet the ego.

* * *

The inner judge is so loud it can drown out our intuition. I found in my own life the first step to silencing the inner judge is to acknowledge it. Then also acknowledge that there is another voice, too. It is a much quieter one, one that is full of wisdom. But, we can't hear that quiet one while our inner judge is screaming at us. So what do we do? I've tried many tactics over the years. I've yelled at it, ignored it, listened to it, tried to change myself, but honestly none of these worked any better than the other. The one that is finally starting to work is understanding where it comes from. The inner judge comes from a place of fear. It comes from a desire for safety, so it doesn't want us to be too big, too bright, or too loud. It thinks that the safest thing to do is to not change and to stay small.

Now that I'm understanding my inner judge's rationale a little more, I have been able to start to give it love. When I feel this judgment come up, I take a step back and ask it, "What fear makes you speak that way? Is that fear real or is it one passed down through generations? Is this judgment even about me?" Now that I am starting to practice discernment, I realize that the judge in my head is more like a lost little child than a mighty tyrant. When I give it compassion, it will settle down and be quiet. Then my inner witness can speak up. It can show me what is needed to move forward. I can learn from my inner judgment instead of being afraid of it.

\* \* \*

## Non-Attachment

The next lesson of the Serpent is Non-Attachment. First, we acknowledge that we write stories about ourselves. Then, we identify the stories that don't serve us and are from a place of fear and scarcity. Now, we must detach ourselves from them. Non-Attachment is the practice of letting go of those roles and stories. What story was assigned to us by our ancestors that is now dictating our lives? What fable have we told ourselves so many times that we believe it to be true? Can we detach ourselves from that story?

Imagine for a minute what it would feel like if you could detach yourself from all these stories. That you, not anyone or anything else, were the sole author of your life story.

Imagine what it would feel like to not be defined by cultural norms, status quos, or what people had told you about yourself. Imagine being free from all of those preconceptions. Being free from all those expectations! The ones you have put on yourself and that others have put on you. Imagine living in a world of discovery and curiosity where you didn't know what tomorrow would bring but you were okay with that. Being free from your attachments to success, money, acceptance, health, and just accepting things as they are right now, with no judgment whatsoever.

Does this sound scary or liberating?

The practice of Non-Attachment is taught by Buddhists, Yogis, and Shamans the world over, because they all understand and acknowledge that attachment is the cause of most of our suffering. Do you ever notice feeling deflated after you've achieved a big goal at work or in life? It's because we are attached to the outcome, not the journey. When the outcome comes and goes, we feel depressed.

This is so common in my running community, where someone runs a big race and then feels depressed in the weeks after. We will put all our energy into achieving that result, and when it's over, we need to find another race to work toward. We move on to the next thing, and the next thing, always looking for satisfaction in the results, and always coming up a little disappointed. Or we can become so attached to the success of something, so afraid of failure, that we won't even take the first step.

The practice of attachment is something that has been deeply ingrained in our patterns and behaviors. Be kind to yourself as you start to walk down the road of non-attachment. Sometimes, just identifying you are attached to something, acknowledging its existence, will help loosen its grip on you. Do this with love, curiosity, and with patience. The practice of non-attachment is a life-long struggle but one worth pursuing.

\* \* \*

# Beauty

The last lesson of the Serpent is beauty. It is acknowledging that everything in life is full of beauty. Sometimes we must search for it, even in the things that we have perceived as ugly. This lesson acknowledges that Mother Earth, Pachamama, The Universal Creator, God, whatever word you want to use, loves unconditionally all of creation. And so all of creation is beautiful in its way. All of it. It's not just what society has defined as beauty. Society says that only the things that shine, look glamorous, or fit in that accepted mold of beauty should be called beautiful. But beauty is not just the rainbows, it is also the thunderstorms.

We can embody beauty in all things and practice that embodiment, even when things are out of balance. Even discord and death are part of nature and so are beautiful in their way. A tornado, a flower, a hummingbird, a human, a spider, a vulture, are all beautiful. A jaguar catching its prey or a lonely child crying for their mother have beauty in them. And so as we look at ourselves with the lens that everything is beautiful, can we also start to love ourselves unconditionally?

43

Maybe that failure you experienced last month is beautiful because it taught you that you needed to do something entirely different. Or that injury you experienced last year is beautiful because it taught you strength and resiliency. If our lives are stories then everything that happens within them is a script. And we can change that script, writing beauty into all of the actions of the play called life.

\* \* \*

## Practice: Finding Beauty

Let's practice finding beauty in our own lives. Write down three things about yourself that you do not find beautiful, that you think are ugly. Now write down three things about other people that you find ugly. Finally, write down three things about the world that you think are ugly.

For example, in the first category, I might write down my large thighs, which do not meet the standard of beauty in our society. The second one I might write down is a person I know who is spiteful and condescending during meetings. The third might be the current war in Ukraine which is full of ugliness, death, and destruction.

Things that you find ugly about yourself

1.
2.
3.

Things that you find ugly about others

1.
2.
3.

Things that you find ugly about the world

1.
2.
3.

So, was that pretty easy to do? We seem to have no problems finding the negative, ugly, or hurtful things in the world.

Now, I want you to find the beauty in these things. This might take a little while and some searching. You may not even be able to find something right now, and that's okay. But keep coming back to these lists. Keep trying to find beauty in them, even when at first glance they seem so ugly.

How are those things about yourself also beautiful?

1.
2.
3.

How are those things about others also beautiful?

1.
2.
3.

How are those things about the world also beautiful?

1.

2.

3.

I will use my examples to help.

My thighs are beautiful because they are strong. They carry me up mountains and have taken me on long runs and hikes. They have helped me to become a runner.

That person I know who has been ugly during meetings is beautiful because I can see her vulnerability and insecurity in her actions. And in seeing that, I have also started to see my insecurities and where she triggers me. I have learned about myself, and have also learned about her through that reflection. I can see that we all struggle in different ways, and so I can find love and beauty for her as a fellow human, each of us just trying our best.

The war in Ukraine—well I needed the words of President Zelenskyy to help me with that one. As I'm writing this book, on December 21, 2022, he spoke to the United States Congress and offered a message of how this suffering and death could also be considered beautiful for the world. No, he didn't use the word beautiful, of course. But it's beautiful because it embodies the courage and conviction in human hearts to defend their loved ones, their homes, their ideals, and their freedom.

He said of the war, "This battle is not only for the territory, for this or another part of Europe. The battle is not only for life, freedom, and security of Ukrainians or any other nation which Russia attempts to conquer. This struggle will define in what world our children and grandchildren will live and then their children and grandchildren. It will define whether it will be a democracy of Ukrainians and for Americans—for all. This battle cannot be frozen or postponed. It cannot be ignored, hoping that the ocean or something else will provide a protection. From the United States to China, from Europe to Latin

America, and from Africa to Australia, the world is too interconnected and interdependent to allow someone to stay aside and at the same time to feel safe when such a battle continues...Ukrainian courage and American resolve must guarantee the future of our common freedom, the freedom of people who stand for their values." Finding beauty in war, a war that has killed many innocent people with no end in sight—that is finding beauty in everything.

\* \* \*

# AYNI

***

# 6

# Understanding our Emotional World

*"The mind is like an iceberg, it floats with one-seventh of its bulk above water."*
– Sigmund Freud

Emotions, what to do with them? We are so good at bottling them up until they explode. We are either repressing them or over-expressing them. Brené Brown's book *Atlas of the Heart* gives names to 87 emotions and experiences! 87! And we need a book like that in our lives. We need to give words to these emotions before we can begin to provide a healthy and balanced expression of them.

In our society, feelings have been downplayed, with thinking, logic, and actions celebrated. We've been told to suppress our feelings; that they make us weak. But if feelings can't be expressed, they go underground. We see outbursts of violence and rage or psychosomatic illnesses. We see the loss of control of our own expression because we don't have names for what we are feeling.

But our feelings and emotions are an intrinsic part of us. No matter what society has told us, we can't just make them go away, nor would we want to. They are as much a part of us as our body and our mind, so we must find a way to make friends with them. Finding healthy expression of our feelings and emotions allows us to come into balance and harmony.

First, I need to differentiate between the words "emotion" and "feeling." Feelings are emotional and physical experiences that we experience daily. They could be hunger, pain, surprise, or frustration. Feelings are something that happens on a conscious level and are transient in nature. They come, and then they go. My shaman teacher would say a feeling is something that lasts for 10 minutes, but if it lasts for days or weeks then it becomes an emotion.

Emotions are below the surface in the unconscious or subconscious mind. Emotions are not experienced immediately the way feelings are, but they inform our belief systems, our desires, and our actions. If a feeling of anger or frustration turns into a lasting emotion, it may lead us to a belief system that the world is a frustrating place and that we are always getting the short end of the stick.

Emotions, since they are below the surface, can be hard to identify or heal, as they are not always known. I like the image of an iceberg to describe feelings vs emotions. The top of the iceberg, the part above water, is what is known and easily identified. These are our feelings. But there is so much below the surface. That is our emotional world. We can spend years, lifetimes even, identifying and working through those emotions and the belief systems they have created. And since feelings and emotions are quite different, I look at them differently in terms of finding balance and harmony with them.

How can we express our feelings in a healthy way for ourselves and others? As we live in a world that is becoming more emotionally aware, this topic is probably not new. Personally, I found yoga especially useful for working through feelings. It's why I started doing yoga all those years ago. I was having such a hard time with the roller coaster of feelings in my life. I would be so happy one day when something good happened, and then a hiccup in life came along and I was despondent. I was a ship in the wild seas being buffeted around with every wave. The practices of yoga - the movement, the breathing, and the meditation practices - all helped me to even out the highs and lows, and to come into more balance and harmony.

The emotions, the ones that have settled into our subconscious, can take a little more work. And you may ask, "Why would we want to unearth them in the first place? They are quite happy down there, underground, deep in the ocean. I'm doing quite well without digging them up, thank you very much." But I can tell you from my own experience that when we bring those emotions to light and really release them from our body, you will feel AMAZING. You will not only feel 100 pounds lighter, but you will have received great treasures and gifts from those revelations.

\* \* \*

## Yogic Approach to Feelings and Emotions

In a yoga workshop I went to many years ago, the Swami talked about feelings. She told us no feeling is "good" or "bad." Each one—anger, jealousy, fear, love, joy—all have things to teach us. The only ones that are pretty much worthless are guilt and shame. They don't serve you, period. End of story. If you did something that you are guilty about, make amends, and then try move on. It serves no further purpose. But the other feelings, even anger and fear, can all help us in their own way. She taught us that we do not need to judge our feelings or call out that we are trying to develop one over another, just to observe them and understand where they come from.

Yoga teachings, especially the ones based on tantra, say all we need to do with our feelings is to develop our witness. The witness is our higher wisdom mind that can look at our experiences with an objective lens. As we develop the witness, when an experience causes a feeling we can step back for a minute and examine that feeling. From that objective lens, we could ask why it is here. Is it because this experience triggered something from the past? Is our feeling related only to what just happened or is it because of an older deeper wound? Based on this feeling, how do we want to respond? Should we scream or should we walk away? We can review the total experience and then choose how we want to express our feeling.

From the witness, we also understand these feelings do not define our identity, and do not have to become deep-seated emotions. Remember, we are so much more. We are all the layers of an onion - the physical body, the emotional body, the mind body, the soul body, and the bliss body. If we feel a pain in our ankle, we do not think that this pain is in our entire body. So if we feel a moment of anger, we do not need to think we are an angry person. If we feel anger about someone cutting in line, do we need to express it? Yes? No? Why? These are questions that maybe you can ask yourself next time a feeling comes up. I do not have the right answer for you, only you do. But I can tell you that if you develop that witness, the right answer will be right in front of you.

As I have developed my witness, it does not mean that feelings stop coming up. I do not become a cool cucumber of non-emotion. I'm just getting better about how I react to those feelings. I observe them and then decide how I will express them. As I write this book, feelings of fear and insecurity come up. I call that voice "my inner mean girl." She says, "Why are you writing this book? No one wants to hear from you. You are not interesting. You have nothing to offer." First, I acknowledge this feeling and give it a moment to express itself in my mind. Fear is often described as F.E.A.R.: False Evidence Appearing Real.

Next, I ask myself, is this a real fear or false evidence appearing real? Is there any evidence that my book is not worth writing? Or that I should abandon the entire project? My mind goes silent. Because no, there is no real evidence, just voices in my head. Do I have to act on this fear? No, I don't. I acknowledge it but choose not to act on it. And when I make that choice, continue writing anyway, and don't feed that feeling anymore, it eventually drifts away.

The yoga practice of yoga nidra is fantastic at helping to develop your witness. It's a process of sense withdrawal that allows your body to relax, which then allows the brain to relax. When the body becomes still, the mind becomes still, and in that stillness, the voice of the witness can be more easily heard. Once you start to know that voice, it becomes easier to hear it when you are in the waking world or when you are in a stressful situation. Through a few deep breaths, you can come back to that place of stillness and find your witness.

The practice of body scanning in the earlier chapter was a short version of yoga nidra. If you'd like to try out a full yoga nidra, you can find recordings on my YouTube Channel. My teacher Swami Muktibodhananda also has several on iTunes or Spotify. Or there are many free recordings by Swami Satyananda or Swami Niranjanananda Saraswati on YouTube. I've included some links to these in the Appendix.

Yoga nidra is also a powerful tool for dealing with the deeper, subconscious emotions. In yoga, these subconscious emotions are called samskaras. Samskara, in Sanskrit, means mental impressions, recollections, or psychological imprints that affect and inform your life. With the iceberg analogy, your samskaras are all of the ice that is below the surface, out of sight. There may have been a trauma that caused you to not feel safe in the dark or to be quick to anger. You may have generational samskaras, passed down from your ancestors. Maybe there was war or suffering in your ancestry—this too affects who you are today.

Samskaras inform and affect our lives in both positive and negative ways. Yoga teaches that the safest way to let go of these samskaras is to practice inner stillness and relaxation. These impressions will then spontaneously come up and be released when they are ready. They are like bubbles, coming up from the deep. When you are in a relaxed state and can be a witness, they just bubble up from time to time and you can then let them go.

A yoga nidra practice includes breathing to relax the mind and body and then will go through a series of visualizations and symbols. These symbols can trigger some of those subconscious emotions and cause them to come up. Our subconscious mind works in symbols, and so a symbol of a red triangle or a blue sky can sometimes bring up a long-buried samskara. If it does, then it is in a place of relaxation and witness so that it can easily be released. It's important to note that when something is released, it should be replaced in your heart with something new and positive. When we break a habit, we are most successful if we replace it with a new and positive habit. Releasing old impressions is the same. If we release the samskara of abandonment and loneliness, we should then invite the idea of friendship and community into our daily life. We empty our cup of the old story of loneliness and fill it with a new one of friendship.

In yoga, it's taught that these imprints will come up when they are ready. It's done with ease and comfort and is, in a sense, a passive process. Other approaches, such as psychotherapy or shamanism, are more active in seeking out these imprints and working through them. If yoga is like the path of water that slowly melts the iceberg, shamanism is a path of fire or rapid transformation. I think both have their place and are fitting for different things. I believe I found shamanism at the time I did because my world was in crisis and I needed a rapid transformation of those emotions. I also believe that I would not have been ready to embrace that transformation without my years of softer and slower healing through yoga.

\* \* \*

## Practice: Breathing Practice – The 4-4-4-4 breath

There are many ways to come to a place of relaxation and stillness – yoga nidra, meditation, and breathing practices. I learned this specific breathing practice in my shamanic training, but it's similar to several pranayama breathing practices I have done in yoga. I even had my Garmin watch lead me in it the other day. The idea of the 4-4-4-4 breath is to slow our breath down which then allows us to slow the body and the mind down. Most people breathe between 12-20 breaths per minute. With this shallow, quick breathing, it's hard for us to step off the hamster wheel of activity and come into a place of stillness. The 4-4-4-4 breath slows our breath down to just four breaths per minute.

Note: If you have asthma or breathing problems, adjust this as is comfortable for you. This should be a comfortable practice that is not a stretch. The point is to slow your breath down from its natural pace, whatever that pace is.

To practice it, come to a comfortable sitting position. Feel your spine straight and tall, and your body relaxed, either in a chair or on the floor on a cushion. Take a few deep breaths in and out. Now, inhale to a count of four (you can mentally count to yourself "In, 2, 3, 4"), hold the breath for a count of four ("Hold, 2, 3, 4"), exhale to a count of four ("Out, 2, 3, 4"), then hold the breath out for a count of four ("Hold, 2, 3, 4"). Repeat this anywhere from five to ten times (one to three minutes). In, 2, 3, 4 - Hold, 2, 3, 4 - Out, 2, 3, 4 - Hold 2, 3, 4. Then take a deep breath in, exhale, and resume normal breathing, spending a few moments in quiet stillness. Observe your thoughts and how you feel, listening to whatever comes up. Note if any messages come to you that are from your higher mind or intuition, or if any feelings or emotions come up that ask for attention. When you feel that you are done with the practice, return to your normal awareness and move your body. Spend a few moments journaling any insights you may have had, or how the experience felt.

Space for Journaling

\* \* \*

# 7

# Facing our Fears

*"The only thing we have to fear is...fear itself"*
*-Franklin D. Roosevelt*

## The Way of the Jaguar

In the Shamanic Medicine wheel, the Jaguar comes to help us into right relationship with our emotions.

The Jaguar is fearless and can walk in the darkest and deepest parts of the jungle. She is strong and powerful, and the rest of the jungle respects her power. She is not afraid of death. She understands the cycle of life but only takes what is needed. In my experience, she is also full of kindness and love, like a mother to her frightened cubs. She shows us in a compassionate way how to be fearless, to be peaceful warriors, and to not be afraid of the dark.

Emotions are imprints on our subconscious. They begin to write our story for us. Our traumas, our past heartbreaks, our perceived failures and successes, our anger, all of these emotions begin to define who we think we are. Jaguar asks us, "Do you want these to always define you?

Or do YOU want to be the one to write your own story?"

In my shamanic teachings, we can offer these emotions, traumas, and feelings to the fire, and let the fire transform them into something greater. Like the stories we mentioned in the previous chapters, we can let them go. They do not need to define us anymore. Our fears, our guilt, our feelings of not being enough, that thing someone said to us we now believe is true, we can let them all go. We can be free to write our own stories of who we are and who we want to be.

Maybe as you've been reading this, one emotion or memory has already come screaming up to the forefront of your mind. You say to yourself, "Yeah this is a toxic one. It is dragging me down and preventing me from living my life. More than anything I would love to let that go. I just don't know how." Let's offer that emotion to the fire!

\* \* \*

## Practice: Fire Ceremony

If you have a limiting belief, story, or emotion that is not serving you and are ready to let it go, we can release it into the fire. The fire will transform its energy, releasing the heaviness back to the Earth and allowing the light to come back into you. What you will need for this practice is a candle, a toothpick, something to put your burnt toothpick in (a small dish or tray), and a quiet space.

Come to your quiet space and light your candle. Bring to the practice a feeling of intention, that this is a ceremony. Intention and ceremony are two critical components of any shamanic practice. Ceremony helps our ancient mind feel into the practice and let it become a part of us. Intention is what makes the magic work. Without it, it's just a candle and a stick.

Now, sitting comfortably, take a long, slow, deep breath in and out, releasing any tension you may have in your body. Take another slow breath in, and exhale any emotional tension. Take a third breath in and release any mental tension. If you are not yet feeling relaxed and centered, continue breathing slowly. With each breath, you can mentally tell yourself on the inhale "I am" and on the exhale "my breath". You can breathe this way for up to two minutes - until you feel that you are ready to put the emotion that is not serving you into the fire.

Now, take the toothpick and bring up to your mind and heart that thing you are ready to let go of. It could be something like, "I am ready to release the anger and heartache from my divorce five years ago," or, "I am done with being anxious every time I leave the house." Take a deep breath and blow the energy of that emotion into the toothpick three times (being careful you don't blow the candle out in the process). Bring intention that you are putting that emotion into the stick and that the fire will take that energy and transform it, releasing you from its hold on your life.

Now, hold the toothpick at one end so you don't burn your fingers, put the other end into the candle flame, and watch the flame slowly burn the stick, releasing whatever feelings are in it.

When the toothpick is mostly burnt, or if your fingers get too hot, put it in the candle or in a small dish to let it finish the process of burning. Now, bring your hands near the fire, gathering up the light and warmth of the flame, and bring that healing light to your stomach, your gut brain. Repeat the process and bring that light to your heart. Now bring your hands one more time to the fire and bring the warmth to the space above your eyes, your eyebrow center, the home of your wisdom and higher mind. Bringing the love and light back into you is a very important part of this ceremony. Nature abhors a vacuum, so whenever we release something from ourselves, we must fill it up with something positive.

Sit with this ceremony for a minute, offering gratitude for the practice and for whatever came up or was transformed. Acknowledge that no feelings or emotions are "good" or "bad" but some may need to be let go to help us step into a more balanced version of ourselves. Then when you are done, snuff out the candle with a plate or cover (do not blow it out) and release the feeling of intention and ceremony.

\* \* \*

## The Way of the Jaguar: A Roadmap to Emotional Freedom

The Jaguar comes to teach us the path of the peaceful warrior, to live a life of fearlessness and full of love. The shamanic teachings of the Jaguar are:

- Fearlessness
- Non-Doing
- Certainty
- Non-Engagement

\* \* \*

## Fearlessness

How do we practice fearlessness? By acknowledging that we have fears and embracing them with love and nonviolence. Being fearless is acting from a place of peace, not from anger or fear. It means developing our own set of ethics and integrity and basing them on our own reality rather than the stories we have been told about reality.

Fear. To be honest, Fear probably guides 95% of the decisions made by 95% of the human population 95% of the time. Maybe I'm exaggerating a tiny bit, but not by much. Fear of losing our job, losing our home, losing our spouse, not doing enough, doing too much, rejection, failure, success, dying, getting sick, the list goes on. And it's not our fault if fear weaves its way so deeply into our subconscious. Watch or read the news, listen to our political discourse, and think about what is talked about in School PTAs, Facebook groups, and community halls. We are taught from day one that this is a world of scarcity and fear. To believe that these messages are not real, that they are F.E.A.R. (False Evidence Appearing Real) takes an awful lot of willpower.

Developing a set of ethics based on our reality and not all that has been fed to us takes a lot of self-reflection and bravery. It is a path to authenticity, fearlessness, and love. Imagine, if we can release these fears and step into the place of fearlessness, we could see that the world is actually a place of abundance and prosperity. This is why we need a jaguar to help us on this path. We need her bravery and her strength. Our fears can paralyze us, and keep us from moving forward. But if we move forward through them, we can understand them, love them, and embrace them. We will see the world in such a different light.

If we aren't motivated by our fears we can be free to let the world unfold as it is meant to. We won't feel the need to control every little detail. We can embrace the joy of discovering the world unfolding. Letting go of our fears is to find freedom and true power. I say this because I have seen it. I have felt it. And yes, facing my fears was one of the hardest things I ever did, but it was worth every single moment.

Here's my story of facing my biggest fear. And how Jaguar came and helped me through that deepest jungle.

* * *

AYNI

My mom was a vibrant healthy 70-year-old. She was happily retired, traveling the world on all sorts of adventures. She'd been everywhere, from the South Pole to Mongolia to Madagascar, and her spirit was unstoppable. In January of 2020, she developed a cough. Maybe it was pneumonia? It got worse as the months progressed. Was it COVID? It was hard to know, because it was during the height of the pandemic and everyone was in lockdown. She took COVID tests—they were negative. She had online telehealth appointments with her doctor but no real diagnosis. Was it allergies? COPD? But she'd never smoked...

She tried different medicines and nothing helped. She was getting more and more out of breath. In September, she finally got an x-ray and CT scan. She had Stage 4 lung cancer. They gave her two years at best and not much in the way of treatment options. But my mom was a fighter. She went into fight mode. We all came together and said we were going to beat this thing. We were going to attack, attack, attack. As the next 10 months of her life unfolded, it was full of hope and despair, trips to the emergency room, going into hospice, going out of hospice, getting experimental treatments, radiating her brain, and finally going back into hospice as the cancer and the treatments left her body broken and in shambles. And yet, she was still not ready to go. She didn't want to die, and I couldn't even begin to understand how someone who had so much life was suddenly leaving us.

And while she was going through all this, I was trying to hold my professional life together. As I helped nurses deliver hospice beds, I was taking calls with my staff working through their construction problems. I was flying back and forth from Colorado to Virginia during the height of COVID, isolating myself to keep her safe. I was managing architectural projects as I managed the aide care, and we all thought if we kept doing, if we kept fighting, we would win. We would conquer cancer through sheer force of will. And when she died, none of it made any sense to me anymore. Life didn't make sense to me anymore. I was

62

devastated. I couldn't understand the point of anything. What was the point of all our doing, and fighting and juggling everything when she still ended up dying anyways?

In my grief, Spirit called me to a piece of paper from the shamanic session I'd done years before. On it was the name of the Four Winds Institute. I found a free masterclass by Dr. Alberto Villoldo where he took us on a journey to find our spirit animal. I remember doing that meditation in my mother's home, as we were planning her memorial and dealing with her estate. And in that meditation, Jaguar came to me. Her black fur wrapped me in love and strength. Her golden eyes told me to not be afraid, and to come on the journey with her. She told me it was time for a change. Later that fall, I signed up for the Four Winds Energy Medicine Training. That spring, our training came into the West Direction, the medicine of the Jaguar, and I knew it was time for me to face my fears.

One of the practices we completed in our training was to face the fear of death by experiencing our own "little" death. This practice was two-fold. First, only in our own death could we be reborn as shamans. Second, it was to understand what death was like, so that we could one day find our way back home when our bodies crossed over. In this practice, the shaman unwinds the chakras and then allows the energetic body to float above the physical body for a short time. They then reattach the energetic body to the chakras, bringing you back to your full self. We were told it was a beautiful experience, where you can experience the joy and light that is found after we die and release from our physical bodies. However, I was PETRIFIED.

My mom's death was not joy and light. It was not a beautiful experience. It was hard, horrible, and painful. She came to my dreams many times after she left, and she was still sad. She wasn't in pain anymore, but there was no joy for her or for me in her passing. Death was not beautiful, it was to be feared. It was to be fought against to the bitter end.

I remember being on one of our video calls in class, talking about how afraid I was of the West Direction, tears running down my face as my teacher gave me comfort and helped me to find the courage to do this practice. My dearest classmate, who I trusted more than anything and who was also terrified, agreed to do the practice with me. And in that "little death," everything changed. When my energy body was lifted out of my physical body, I felt lighter than I had ever felt. I felt freedom from all the things that had been weighing me down–my grief, my traumas, and my fears. I just WAS. I was part of something bigger, universal, and it was love, and it was light.

Everything I had thought about death had been wrong. It was not something to be avoided or run away from. It was just part of the cycle of things. It did not have to be full of pain and sadness only, it could also be full of love. The grief of mom's passing turned from the devastating pain of fear and loss to a beautiful pain, the pain of love not having an earthly outlet. The world past death was not a place of fear. And if even death wasn't something to be afraid of, then what was left in life to fear?

As I went through my shamanic training, I was later able to help my mother with her own energetic death rites. I brought her soul back to this plane for a few moments, and with my classmates' help, we released her from her place of sadness and into the realm of love and light. It was perhaps the most beautiful thing I've ever done in my life.

So, dear reader, what are your biggest fears?

Many sages would say the biggest fear we have is the annihilation of the Ego, of losing ourselves and becoming part of something bigger. But in the same breath, the yogis talk about this as a transcendental experience, where we are one with everything. To them, this is the whole purpose of their practice, to experience that bliss of oneness. The soul is so excited about this idea, but the Ego is like, "Nope, no thanks. I'm good. Let's just stay as we are." And so it fabricates FEAR with a capital F. The fear of death, or of losing our "I" - ness.

But when I really experienced it in that practice, I found it wasn't so scary after all. Instead of destroying me, it brought me a great gift. It brought me the realization that death was not the end. It made me realize that I am part of a bigger world, and that world was full of love and light.

I invite you to ask yourself, what can you do to begin to walk down the path of fearlessness? Are you currently in a place that is full of fear, anxiety, or stress? I hope not, but if you are, could this moment become an opportunity to transform that fear into feelings of love and light? Our crises and traumas can be places of great fear, but also places of great opportunity. The most important thing is to look at them with love and non-judgment. Ask them how they can help us be opportunities. Befriend them. Show them compassion, and then ask them if they are False Evidence Appearing Real.

However, you don't have to do this transformation on your own. I transformed these fears with the support and love of my entire shaman class and our many practice healing sessions. We practiced MANY times as we released these fears. I went through it by talking to a grief counselor who gave me permission to feel exactly what I was feeling. I went through it by talking with my loved ones. In my own meditations, I went through these feelings with jaguar by my side. The most important thing is to know that it can be done. That you can transform your fears and step into a place of fearlessness. That you can walk with jaguar into the darkest jungles, because you are never alone, and she will be your light in the darkness. And if you need help, find a shamanic practitioner, a therapist, a friend, or reach out to me! I am happy to help! We all need a little help sometimes, especially when we are in dark places.

And if you aren't feeling anything come up as I go through these stories that is okay, too. Trust that the Universe will give you opportunities to process your emotions as you are ready to handle them. Don't try to force them. That will only cause stress and anxiety, and we already have plenty of that in our lives.

Now ask yourself, when a situation comes up again in your life, what will it look like to respond to it from a place of peace? Can you respond to it with love and compassion and not anger or fear? Every time we successfully do this, we get better and better at it. Because every time we do something successfully, then we "know" we can do it. And then it's easier to do it again.

When the news comes on, when the politics tell you that the world is doom and gloom, stop and question that reality. Is this the way the world needs to be? Remember the idea of Ayni. Just because we have been taught this reality of scarcity and fear, it does not mean that it's the only way the world needs to unfold. The future has not yet been written. We do not have to take the story that has been handed to us by the people in charge or by the past generation. We can be the storytellers as much as anyone else.

The practice of fearlessness also means developing your own set of ethics and then living by them. It is not blindly accepting the views of society or the story that has been written for you. So many of us are taught from a very young age to be completely UN-certain about everything we think and feel. We look for external validation for our feeling, our beliefs, and our morals. To practice fearlessness, we need to find and embrace our own story and our own beliefs.

This issue came up as I was trying to think about why I'm qualified to write this book. I feel no better or worse qualified than anyone else. Though I am sharing my personal experience, it should not dictate what you feel or experience. For I am just one person in a world of eight billion. I am no greater than a blade of grass, no more than a pebble in a sea of pebbles. I am not a shaman from a long line of shamans or a yogi who has lived in an ashram for years. And even if I was, it wouldn't make a difference, because I'm asking you to create your own set of stories and beliefs, and not to adopt mine.

The consensual reality tells us that others are better than us and we should look to 'experts' or other people to tell us how to be and what to feel. But this is not entirely true. They cannot tell you how to feel any more than a shaman can. They can offer you teachings, or show you practices, but they cannot change your world for you. Only you can do that. A wise shaman would say I can show you the path, but you must be the one to walk it. You must be the one to explore how you feel. You must be certain in your own convictions and experiences.

We are all just pebbles, in the sea of pebbles, but if you want we can take a stand and say, "No! I want to be fearless! I want to write a new story!" And if you take that stand with me, then we are two pebbles in that sea of pebbles.

Now, if you want to develop a new set of beliefs and ethics, could they be ethics about Ayni? About a world of interconnectedness and joy and abundance, instead of the story we are told about scarcity and fear? What does that story feel like to you? Try it on, and see how it fits. Feel empowered to write your new story.

It's okay to question what we've been taught. It's also okay to accept certain societal norms. They keep our society from falling into disarray and chaos. But still question them. It's also okay to not buy into what everyone else is doing. Truthfully, what everyone else is doing is killing the planet and causing divisiveness in our society. It is time for us to be fearless and start developing a new set of ethics and integrity, ones that are in alignment with our hearts and our higher purpose. And that has to start with ourselves.

\* \* \*

# Non-Doing

Non-Doing is the idea of coming into the flow of the Universe, instead of forcing our will on it. It is being in the present and not two steps into the future. It's the idea of letting things unfold in their own time and not forcing things into action.

During my shamanic training, this idea of non-doing was completely alien to me. I had ingrained in my brain the adage, "Don't put off until tomorrow what you can do today." In my mind, the practice of non-doing was just another name for laziness and procrastination. It went against everything I had been taught in my life.

But this practice is key to finding Ayni and that harmonious relationship with yourself and the planet. Why? Because at its very core is acknowledging that there is a flow of the Universe and that you are part of the flow. It is not about inaction. It's about rightly timed action.

I have been practicing architecture for 20 years. In the last three years since the COVID Pandemic, NOTHING has worked right. We have had supply chain issues, contractor issues, labor issues, more supply chain issues, more labor issues—it has been virtually impossible to get a project built under any sort of schedule. I put so much energy into forcing things to happen. I would do, and do, and do some more, but I felt like we still didn't get anywhere. All my doing accomplished very little. It didn't change the schedules. It didn't make things work better. It just created more stress and anxiety. Do you recognize this story anywhere in your life? If so, do you want to try out the practice of non-doing?

I finally realized that this endless frustration was the Universe telling me it was time to take a step back from architecture and put my energy into something else (like writing this book). It was telling me to do something more in alignment with my heart. It wanted me to stay in the present and to let things unfold within the flow of the Universe. Now I'm not telling you to quit your job and go on a vision quest, but I am inviting you to find those places in your life that are calling out for a little bit of non-doing. You will be surprised at what happens on its own when you stop forcing it.

When we take ourselves out of the equation and come into the flow, then synchronicities begin to happen. Like the synchronicity of me finding that shaman healer on vacation, or that book that gave me the courage to run. Or the synchronicity of me finding an electric car in stock the exact week I decided it was time for me to get an electric car, even though people had been on wait lists for months.

The Universe will unfold exactly as it chooses; we can either fight it or get into the flow.

* * *

## Practice: Practicing Non-Doing

I invite you to practice this idea of non-doing in your life. Think of something that you have been fighting and forcing to happen but just isn't coming out right. Write it down here, so you can come back and look at it later.

Now make a conscious effort to let it be for two days, two weeks, or a month. And as you make that effort, say a little prayer to the Universe. Say mentally, with intention, "I surrender the outcome of this task to the Universe. I trust that the Universe will reveal to me the path forward at the right time. I believe in synchronicity and am open to letting the Universe guide me in this task."

You may be very surprised at what unfolds on its own.

\* \* \*

## Certainty

The practice of certainty is really about having faith in yourself and in the course you have chosen. If your heart is calling you to a certain path, it's about walking that path without having any back doors or escape routes. It is being fully engaged and committed. There's no going back because there is no need. You have absolute trust in Spirit and the Universe.

Often, when we decide to do something, we give ourselves lots of escape routes, just in case things don't work out. The trouble with these is that they keep us from putting our whole heart into that thing. Now I want to be clear, there's a difference between full commitment and jumping off a cliff without a parachute. If you're going to make a big life change, it's perfectly reasonable to make sure you have your finances in order, consider the relationships and people you value, and ensure that you have put some thought and care into your plan of action. We live in this world and the world has certain rules.

But, and this is a big but, we can't let these details prevent us from ever walking down the path of certainty. Certainty asks us to be committed to our journey, no matter what. Yes, this may sound scary, but commitment and certainty can be scary! Anyone who has made a life-long commitment to a spouse, a child, or a job, can understand how much fears those commitments can bring up. All of the What-ifs, and the might-have-been. But they also know how rewarding these commitments can be in the long run.

It's like a marriage, but to yourself. You are 100% committed to taking care of yourself, for richer or poorer, in sickness and in health. You are not going to keep cheating on yourself with your old partners; you deleted all their numbers and unfriended them on social media. Trust in yourself, trust in Spirit, trust that the Universe has your back and that you will be taken care of. Trust that the Universe is unfolding just as it should. That you are part of the bigger plan, not some aberration. And trust that you are here, right now, reading this sentence for a reason. If all those are true, then you don't need a back door or escape route, because you are already on the right path.

I had a few dreams about this as I was starting to walk down my path of shamanism. They brought up all those insecurities, but they also showed me the hope, joy, and possibility that would come if I practiced certainty. In my waking life, though I had those dreams as guides, I had to take them and manifest them into my reality. I knew that it was time for me to step back from my current job and start living in Ayni. I knew it was time to shed the stories I was holding onto, the fear of the unknown. My husband was supporting my journey, he was ready to sacrifice our lifestyle and routine, but I was still holding myself back. And so the Universe kept sending me signs, louder and louder ones, making me more and more miserable, until I was ready to surrender to certainty. Finally, I yielded! I said to myself, *"Fine! I give up! I quit!"*

I put my finances in order, was grateful that I had the opportunity to do so, and made a big life change. I quit my job, closed the escape routes, and opened myself up to the Universe. Everyone told me I was brave for following my dreams, but I don't think it was being brave. It was me giving up control, it was me surrendering. Pure and complete surrender. But surrender is not failure, it's just finally letting go of the reins. Surrender is the secret that all the sages of the world teach as the greatest lesson. Full and complete surrender to the Universe is what leads you to your highest destiny.

\* \* \*

## Practice: Feeling into Certainty

Journaling Exercise: Sit for a few moments and think about your heart's biggest desire and what course it might take you. For example, as I write this book my heart's desire is to live in Ayni and to help others live in Ayni.

What is your heart's biggest desire?

Now, write down all the things that you are doing in pursuit of this desire. If you haven't done them yet, write down what you plan to do.

1.
2.
3.

Now, write down all the things that are back doors, escape hatches, things that aren't really in alignment with this goal, but make you feel comfortable.

1.

2.

3.

Ask yourself, can I stop doing them? If you say no, really ask why. Is it fear? Is it timing? Be honest with yourself, and see if there are any changes that you could make in your life to help you practice certainty. And if there are things outside of your control that prevent you from stepping into certainty, give them to the Universe. Ask for help, and that the path forward be revealed to you in the right time.

\* \* \*

## Non-Engagement

Jaguar's last lesson is another tough one, at least it was for me. Did I mention in the beginning that our emotional side is challenging to work through? It sure is for me, and every time I go back through these practices, I find new little gems that have been hiding deep in the jungle of my subconscious.

If you have watched politics in the U.S. over that last 10 years, you know that non-engagement is not a practice used very much. Attack, attack, attack is the language of the land. More recently, it has become if someone goes low, we should go lower. We are in a race to the bottom in our society in terms of divisiveness and emotional violence. And this translates into physical violence—mass shootings, road rage, suicides, and abuse. How can we break free from this cycle?

In my personal practice, non-engagement is one that I have to come back to again and again. At first, I thought this practice was just don't engage. When someone ticks you off, turn the other cheek and don't respond. I guess this is a good start. I encourage you to practice this as a start, as that's how I started. Now to be clear, non-engagement does not mean letting yourself become a doormat for people to walk over. It means that when faced with a battle or skirmish in your life, you choose not to engage in it. It could be walking away, withholding that last word to prove you are right, or not honking the horn at the person that cut you off.

In time, practicing non-engagement can also help us discover that the triggers which make us want to engage. These triggers are actually little gems in our subconscious, waiting to be discovered and healed. They are mirrors into our shadow side.

Think of the people that you can't help but fight with. When my step-children were growing up, one of them was easy going but the other was in constant battle mode. We often failed as parents, because when he pushed our buttons, we would engage. We would engage because we were the adults and had to prove our points, because we wanted him to conform to our expectations, and wanted to control the outcome of the situation. He engaged because he wanted to be his own independent self, and wanted to control his destiny. Looking back, I can see it was a lose/lose battle and not worth our collective energy. Our energy would have been so much better spent in trying to understand why he saw the world so differently, and how we could help him navigate his experience, not wasting it on screaming and yelling.

My husband and I are also both strong willed people, and often engage in little battles. They could be battles of control and power that truthfully stemmed from hurt feelings and wanting to be seen and heard. When I first started to practice the work of non-engagement, I came into it on a high horse of superiority. I thought to myself, here he is trying to create a skirmish; I will just not engage. I will sit quietly until he has exploded all his anger. Because then I am "enlightened" and he is just living in his "emotions." HA! What a joke that was on me. It was not honest or authentic. Violence still lived within me—I was just pretending it didn't. Shutting down is not the same as not-engaging; it's being passive-aggressive.

To get into an authentic place of non-engagement, I had to do some more soul-searching and healing. I had to learn why I was being triggered. I had to come into a place of non-violence within myself before I could stop engaging in the battles around me. The path of the peaceful warrior is one that looks at the world through a lens of love and compassion. It doesn't mean that they don't stand up for themselves or that they don't ever engage in a battle, but they pick their battles carefully and battle from a place of love, not anger.

If you struggle with this one, like I did, give yourself some grace. We are all just trying, fumbling around, attempting to make sense of a world that really didn't give us a guidebook, and listening to feelings and emotions that we have been blocking out for lifetimes. Every time we have success in something, we will be able to do it again and again. And the more we practice, the better we get.

As we heal our emotional traumas, little by little, we begin to see that maybe, just maybe, we are a beautiful being that is full of love and light.

In fact, I already know that you are. Most of us have people that see us for the beautiful humans that we are, but we can't see it in ourselves. We have told stories about ourselves that we believe are true. That we are not good enough, that we are ugly, stupid, we don't look right, and that our feelings are bad. These stories have buried themselves deep in our heart and our being, but that doesn't make them true. It's time to unbury them, to release them to the fire. Let them go, so that you can transform. We have all been caterpillars, and it's time to become a butterfly.

One of the yoga 'deities' I have always been attracted to is Kali. She represents a strong and violent feminine force. She's depicted as a fierce woman with black skin and a bright red tongue and carries in her four hands a sword, a trident, the head of a demon she killed, and a bowl to collect the demon's blood. She is fierce and relentless as she destroys the demons that prevent humanity from achieving full realization. But Kali is not just a bloodthirsty goddess, she is also a peaceful warrior, and embodies the way of the jaguar. She is fearless and strong. She uses her power to slay the demons and the darkness within us so that we can step into the light. She has a nurturing and creative aspect and understands that in order for new things to be born, others must die.

I invite you to embrace your Kali, your jaguar. I invite you to step fearlessly into the dark places and find the gems within. To walk the path of becoming a peaceful warrior. A warrior who will use their sword to slay fears and insecurities. A warrior will use their sword, not in violence, but to weed out the garden so that you can plant seeds of love and beauty and peace in your soul.

* * *

# 8

# We are all Energy

*"Everything is energy, and that's all there is to it."*
*–Albert Einstein*

We have spent some time working on our relationship with our bodies and emotions. Now let us travel into the more subtle parts of ourselves. In yoga, these would be called the mental, intuitive, and bliss koshas. The first step to coming into a balanced relationship with these is acknowledging that our mind is more than just our Ego. We explored how to start listening to our witness and higher mind. Maybe you have started to hear that witness in your own life.

First of all, I want to say, congratulations! You are hearing your true, authentic self! Even if we only hear it occasionally, it's still something to celebrate. This is you! And isn't it lovely? Our higher mind, our souls, can be full of love and peace and calm and wisdom. And take a moment to realize this is YOU. It's not something outside of you on a throne somewhere. It's just beautiful, authentic, miraculous YOU.

The second step is understanding that our minds exist in a larger framework we call the Universe. We are not a static and individual entity removed from it—we are part of the bigger reality. We can choose to be a part of that reality, moving through it in flow and harmony. Or we can try to shape it to our own will and desire, which in the end only causes suffering and mental anguish. It's like the story about finding the outfit in the shopping mall. When we try to impose our will on reality instead of working within the flow, we only find more suffering.

And so, we ask, how do we get into the flow? Can the voice inside us help us to better understand the world outside of us? Can it help us to understand our place in the world and see the bigger plans of the Universe? To see our highest path, our purpose in life? Can we connect with the Universal Consciousness? That which is both beyond us and within us? Maybe we can achieve those moments of bliss the yogis talk about, where we are part of everything and everything is part of us. Maybe we can start realizing a world of Ayni.

My answer is Yes. Yes, we can.

In the many years I studied yoga theory they would talk about the "bliss body," that part of us that is connected with everything in the Universe. Swamis would describe their meditations where they would cease to exist, as they dissolved into the Universe. This was called samadhi, or bliss. In Buddhism, they call it Nirvana, and Buddhists describe it as the state where we cease to be an individual and merge with the Universe. It's a place of full peace and surrender. In my shamanic teachings, this is the aspect of the eagle. It is flying above everything, where you can see the whole curve of the Earth or narrow down to see the smallest mouse. It's a place of both-and, not either-or. It's a place where you are part of everything and everything is part of you. As above, so below. As without, so within.

If we can come up to that place, then we can see ourselves in the bigger fabric of the Universe, and how can play our part. We see the bigger picture and get perspective on the pain and suffering in our world right now. We can even see how that suffering is part of the bigger unfolding of the Universe. We see a way forward to a place of Ayni - of reciprocity, balance, and harmony.

As I went around the medicine wheel in my shamanic training, I began to imagine what this might be like, but never personally experienced it. It seemed like such an amazing thing! After all, sages and prophets had spoken about it for thousands of years. Then one day, I experienced this bliss, and have had glimpses after that. Each glimpse is the most precious gift. It is said that very few people can stay in this place of bliss, but even just a glimpse is inspiring enough to alter the course of our lives. I feel that if we could all see that glimpse, it would be so obvious to us how we can come into a place of love and giving - for ourselves, each other, and the planet.

I want to share my experiences with you because though they are only my experiences, I hope they inspire you to pursue this deeper exploration. They keep me going through the dark times. Even when we feel isolated and alone, sometimes just knowing in our hearts that we are all connected is enough to get us through life's challenges.

My first experience was in a yoga retreat. We were doing the practices of Kriya Yoga and Tattwa Shuddhi. These are advanced practices that can only be taught by someone initiated by their guru. I am honored I have been able to practice these powerful techniques. Kriya Yoga is the Yoga of action and awareness. Tattwa shuddhi, in Sanskrit, means the purification of 'thatness'. It is the purification of that which is our identity - our body, mind, and soul - so that we can experience our existence within the bigger fabric of the Universe.

In my retreat, we worked on these each day for the entire week. My body resisted the practices. Each time I started to go deep it would revolt, creating an ache somewhere, or start bobbing around trying to fall asleep. Then the last day, just as it was about to topple over, Swamiji said, "Now put your body in a psychic lock. Tell it to be still, so that your energetic body can be released." Somehow that was exactly the message I needed. I told my body to be still and then POOF, my energetic body released and went outside the room. It was one with the trees and the birds that were flying around and the wind and the sun. It was connected with all those things. I was still me but not me. I was more than me; I was a part of everything. I realized that the chickadee and the tree and the moss and the stone were all part of the Universe, just as I was. I understood I was not better, or superior, to them. I was as much alive as they were and they were as alive as me. We were all consciousness and we were all energy. It was the most incredibly beautiful, loving experience.

Many months later, I had another experience during the same yoga practice of tattwa shuddhi. I had been continuing my healing journey, releasing my fears and stories, and felt much lighter in my soul. During the practice, I sent my awareness all the way up to the energy point of Sahashrara, the energy center that connects us with the Universe. As I lifted into this vast Universe, as far as I could see was blackness. The entire Universe was blackness. But the blackness was filled with an infinite number of pinpoints of light. I somehow knew these pinpoints were the energy that was the building blocks of all things. Like the subatomic particles that will eventually make up atoms, which then make up molecules, which then make up cells, and eventually make us. But in their most basic form, they are just energy. They don't know yet what kind of atom they will be. And in my vision, though I did not see it, there was an understanding that consciousness is what tells that energy to be. That the two are entwined, consciousness and energy. That neither exists without the other. Without consciousness, it's just energy floating in the dark infinite. And without energy, consciousness cannot take form. And in this realization, I realized that we ARE all connected, because we are all the same basic building blocks of energy. At a very basic level, we are all the same, and it's only consciousness which differentiates us.

This is one of the ideas behind quantum physics. Physics studies these building blocks of energy and is starting to understand how they are all connected. The Nobel Prize for physics this year went to scientists who proved the idea of entanglement, that particles separated by space can still affect each other's movements. Take that in for a moment. It has been proven by science that particles are connected, even when they are separated by distance. Could quantum physics also be called Spirit? It is just a word after all. The idea of Universal Energy, Interconnectedness, and Universal Consciousness are what Shamans, Yogis, and Buddhists have been talking about for a few thousand years.

Energy is universal. Every creature, every star, every water droplet is created with the same energy. And consciousness gives it form. Maybe it is our consciousness or will, maybe it's a universal consciousness, or maybe they are the same thing. The great Greek philosopher Hermes Trismegistus wrote "As above, so below, as within, so without, as the universe, so the soul."

To me, this idea of interconnectedness is at the root of everything. Its absence is at the root of our suffering. When we feel isolated and alone, or don't feel a connection with our fellow man or animal, we suffer. We feel that they are "other," and perceive others as threats, not allies. We feel justified in our actions of taking and hoarding because it's Us vs. Them. We believe this world is based on either-or, and that it's "every man for himself." But I think so many of us are tired of suffering and feeling alone, unsupported, and isolated. We are tired of the rat race, the hamster wheel, and all the other metaphors and analogies that describe this world of scarcity and fear. So many of us are yearning for connection, love, and support.

And so that is why I share my experiences. Even if you have not yet experienced the true interconnectedness of everything, perhaps just dreaming of it is a good start. Our most powerful force is our intention.

If we really yearn for something, if we put our thought, will, and heart behind it, then the Universe will show us the path to finding it.

That is what happened to me. I yearned for this connection, and the Universe gave me the teachings of yoga and shamanism to show me the way. I yearned for happiness, love, and light in my life, and it showed me the bliss of interconnectedness. It showed me Ayni, that we are all connected and that what we do affects each other in the most powerful way.

\* \* \*

## Shiva and Shakti

In yoga, what I experienced in that vision could also be called Shiva and Shakti. Shiva is the nothingness that is the universal consciousness, and Shakti is the energy that fuels everything. The black void and the pinpricks of light. The ancient yogis understood that the two were inseparable. Their union is what creates life. They are represented as male and female forces, with the female being the creative energy and the male being the consciousness. Without the feminine force, the masculine force is inert. Without consciousness, energy doesn't have a shape. To come into right relationship with ourselves and with the world, we need BOTH aspects.

This is where our society has struggled. We've been living in a patriarchal society for a very long time. Even India, where yoga originated, has become a patriarchy. The feminine has been downplayed, suppressed, and abused. And so our relationship with Shakti, the divine creative force is a bit of a mess. To be honest, our relationship with Shiva, the divine masculine force is also a bit of a mess. We see so many examples of toxic masculinity, misuse of power, and violence; these are not the divine masculine. Just as the wounded feminine—meek, quiet, subjugated - is not the divine feminine. To come into right relationship with both, we need to find the healthy aspects of both - within ourselves, and within the world. But how do we do this? What road maps are there to come back to this right relationship?

The ancient Yoga Patanjali Sutras offer a path to achieve this interconnectedness of things. They call it samadhi or bliss, where the "I" ceases to exist and you are a part of the Universal Consciousness. This path is called Ashtanga – or the Eightfold Path. These practices are at least 2000 years old and have stood the test of time, so they must have some serious wisdom in them. It is said that if you follow these practices with discipline and regularity, you will be able to achieve samadhi. Here's a quick summary:

- Yamas – These are a list of ethical rules to live by and include practicing non-violence, truthfulness, non-stealing, restraint, and non-possessiveness
- Niyamas - These are a list of habits to incorporate into your life and include purity, contentment, self-discipline, self-study, and spiritual contemplation
- Asana – yoga postures to allow meditation to be steady and comfortable
- Pranayama – Breathing practices to begin to control the breath and our energy
- Pratyahara – Sense withdrawal to bring the mind within. Yoga nidra is a practice of pratyahara
- Dharana – single pointed focus. This is something often done after yoga nidra or part of a meditation practice
- Dhyana – Meditation that is uninterrupted contemplation. Easier

said than done!
• Samadhi – Achieving Bliss! Union with the Universe!

It is said that if you practice all of these diligently, you will achieve that moment when your "I" -ness disappears and you are just a part of the Universe. But, like most things, yoga teaches you can't jump to the end. All of these pieces are required to achieve a balanced and authentic experience.

Does the idea of achieving bliss sound exciting to you? If so, you may want to start deepening your practice of yoga. It can be harder than you think to find yoga studios that teach all of these, but if you are sincere in your quest, I am sure the Universe will assist you. I was fortunate that I found the Bihar School of Yoga and the teachings of Swami Satyananda which teach yoga in terms of this holistic approach. I say fortunate, but I also know that there is no such thing as coincidence.

I want to share another eightfold path or Asthanga. This one has also been near and dear to my heart for many years, and has been a personal road map for me.

Swami Sivananda was a guru who was born at the turn of the 19th Century. He went on to be the guru of Swami Satyananda who founded the Bihar School of Yoga. Swami Sivananda's eightfold path was based on karma yoga, which is the yoga of service. The path is a simple one. Serve, Love, Give, Purify, Be Good, Do Good, Meditate, and Realize. He wrote that these practices were a roadmap to peace and harmony. To me, this roadmap also sounds very much like Ayni.

You start with service, because in service you will find love and compassion for those you help. When you find love, it will be natural for you to want to share that love with others. In sharing your love and giving selflessly, you will purify your heart. Purification will lead you to want to be good and to do good for others and the planet. When you are in this place of service and giving and are pure of heart, meditation will come without effort. And in that meditation, you will realize the interconnectedness of everything. You will find peace and harmony.

In 2014, I went to the Satsang Ashram in Deoghar for the Sat Chandi Maha Yajna. It's a 5-day fire ceremony to uplift humanity and bring peace, prosperity, and happiness into people's lives. Every day we sang kirtan (a call and response type of chant), listened to lectures, and participated in the fire ceremony. The ashram gave gifts to the people of the village from bags of rice to rickshaws. In fact, about the only thing we didn't do was yoga asana postures.

All the visitors did seva, or service. I woke up at Four each morning to clean the ashram, then my seva was to pour a small jug of water to wash the hands of the thousands who had come for the meals as part of the celebration. It was an intense and emotional experience to have such intimate contact with so many.

There was so much love shared during these five days. As we sang the chants of kirtan, our hearts soared in love, and we felt love for everyone in the ashram. This ceremony was an embodiment of Swami Sivananda's eightfold path. The ashram was generous in its giving to the people of the village. The Swamis showed us how to be good and do good. They gave us a map of how we could live our lives through service and love. We were also purified as part of the fire ceremony, and it elevated the energy level for all participants. It was a life-changing event for me, one that changed my entire trajectory.

I invite you to take these ideas into your own life. Practice being of service first, and see where it leads you. It was hard during COVID for many of us to volunteer. We became inner focused, but it is time for us to build back into a community of giving. I invite you to find a place or organization you are passionate about and volunteer your time. Use your skills or just your hands and serve. Or if you don't know of an organization, just help a stranger. Strike up a conversation with someone that you see and ask if they need help. Maybe they will say no, but I bet they will appreciate being asked.

\* \* \*

## The Eagle and the Swami

I want to share another vision I had not long after that beautiful meditation of the cosmos full of pinpricks of light.

*I closed my eyes and grounded myself, feeling the Earth and the plants and all the microorganisms that are alive. I was one with all of those living things, sitting quietly on the earth. Out of nowhere my guru came to me in a hot air balloon. He invited me into the balloon. He told me that I'd been spending too much time down on the ground and I needed to come up higher for perspective.*

*He took me up into the air, above the atmosphere, almost into space. Then, a great eagle flew up alongside us. The Eagle, a symbol from shamanism, and my yoga guru, together on the same journey. It was the coming together of both traditions. We looked at the whole planet below us. We saw the pain and suffering, the areas that had been burnt by fire and devastation. I was full of sadness seeing the burnt area, but then they told me to look to the horizon. And I could see also forests of trees, each individual tree breathing life back into the planet. They showed me that death and life are both there and will always be there. They also showed me that yoga and shamanism are both there and will always be there. I understood that my path was never going to be EITHER-OR, yoga or shamanism, architect or healer, but BOTH-AND. For it was in the coming together, the integration, that we can truly understand the connectedness of things.*

And so, maybe that is why I am writing this book with both yoga and shaman teachings, and a sprinkling of architecture. They are all a part of me and all a part of the world. Just the sheer idea that yogis and shamans 2000 years ago, continents apart, were teaching the same thing shows that there is a universal truth in their wisdom.

The world is full of both pain and joy, death and life, just as I saw it from that hot air balloon. And so are we. We are pain and joy and death and rebirth, both-and, not either-or. When we can come into acceptance of that in ourselves, we can see it in each other and the planet.

\* \* \*

# AYNI

***

# 9

# Learning to Fly

*"The best and most beautiful things in the world cannot be seen or touched.*
*They must be felt with the heart."*
*-Helen Keller*

## The Teachings of Hummingbird and Eagle

The Medicine Wheel, as taught by the Four Winds Institute, has in the North Direction - the level of Spirit, the archetype of a hummingbird. The hummingbird can help us find our soul's path, to encourage us to go on the great journey. Hummingbirds fly great distances while only sipping on the nectar of flowers. They are a reminder for us to find our courage and embark on our journey even when we don't think we can. They remind us to not waste time on the junk of life but to feed only on the sweet nectar of love and beauty.

The archetype of condor or eagle is in the East Direction, the energetic level and the place of the rising sun. Eagle represents our connection with the energy that is greater than us, and helps us take that higher perspective in life. Eagle teaches us to soar high above ourselves, our ego, everything that makes us an individual, and come into connection with the higher Universe.

I put both hummingbird and eagle teachings in this chapter because, for me, they have been tied so closely together that it's difficult to pull them apart. As I connect with my spiritual nature, there's a natural progression to a place of higher wisdom. When we realize we are all energy, the energy between us and the rest of the world starts to blur together.

These are subtle practices and teachings. I don't know that we can put a ton of 'effort' into exploring our energetic and soul natures. This is a place of "being", not "doing." It requires a humble acknowledgment that it will happen exactly when and how it's supposed to.

We began the practice of non-doing in the teaching of jaguar and continue. We must surrender our Ego to find our soul's purpose and its connection with the Universe. In that surrender, we can begin to see the world from that higher perspective and how we fit into it.

The Practices of the Hummingbird are:

- Invisibility / Transparency
- Keeping a Secret
- Beginners Mind
- Living Congruently

The Practices of Condor / Eagle are:

- Indigenous Alchemy
- Owning our Projections
- No Mind
- Mastery of Time

These practices are a lot to unpack. They are practices that will take you down the path of becoming a shaman, one that is in complete connection with nature and walks in the realm of the invisible and the visible. At the risk of sounding dismissive, I will say it's not necessary that you master all of these to begin to live in Ayni or to come into right relationship with the planet. It's not that these aren't incredible practices, these are practices we can spend a lifetime on. But I don't want everyone to think they must be master practitioners to begin to make a difference in the world. We do not need to be enlightened or have reached "bliss" to know that it is out there and that we should work to achieve it for all living things. We just need to reach for it, and in that reaching, we will already be acting in a place of love for ourselves.

So, as I touch on these ideas, if any light a spark within you, I encourage you to look for teachers and deeper training that will help support you on this journey. That spark may be calling you to become a shaman, healer, or earth keeper. Maybe it's time for you to really begin your soul's journey.

\* \* \*

# The Way of the Hummingbird

## Invisibility

The Idea of Invisibility / Transparency is to understand that the true authentic you is more than all the roles in life you have adopted and defined yourself by for most of your life. Take a moment, get out a piece of paper, and write down all the roles that you have. If I was to do this I would write down Architect, Step-mother, Wife, Shaman,

Author, Yogi, Runner, Daughter, Sister, Problem Solver, Listener, etc., etc.

Now, what if we threw all those out? What if we offered each one to the fire? What is the "you" that is beyond all your roles? If you want to give it a try, do so! Take those roles to the fire. Have a little fire ceremony, write those all on small pieces of paper, or blow them into a toothpick and offer each one to the fire. As you bring the light of the candle flame or the fire back into your heart, ask for wisdom to understand the "You" that is beyond all of those roles. Get to know your 'soul'. Then, become invisible, even to yourself.

\* \* \*

## Keeping a Secret

This is the idea that deep inside we already know that we are co-creators of the Universe, and that we have all of the wisdom of the Cosmos within us. But we keep it a secret, even from ourselves.

There is a story in India about the deity Krishna. When he was a little boy, he opened his mouth wide to his mother. Inside Krishna's mouth she could see the entire Universe. But it was too overwhelming for her to see the entire cosmos inside her son, so he made her forget it. And this is why it's a secret that we know, but keep from ourselves. Because it's such a profound truth, we can't just walk around with it on our t-shirt.

This idea of keeping a secret was a huge one for me. Like HUGE, cried all over the place, had my heart burst into little pieces, huge. Let me explain.

Shamanism teaches that we were never kicked out of the Garden of Eden. That there is God within us, for we are the embodiment of God's source energy. It teaches that we have the power of creation within us and can be co-creators with the Universe. It's not saying that we are all little Gods and can do whatever we want; that would be a recipe for disaster. It's saying we can CO-create with the Universe. We can understand the bigger flow, how we fit into it, and what our heart's purpose is. Then we start manifesting that into reality. I found this one hard for me to take in. It's easy to think that Krishna had the entire Universe within his mouth, that Buddha or Gandhi or Mohammed or Jesus did, but not me. Deep down I still feel flawed. I don't feel that I have 'God' within me. I can understand intellectually the idea that we are all co-creators of the Universe, but feeling it was a whole different matter.

I asked my teacher about this during my shamanic training, and she offered me the following wisdom. She said "Maybe this idea is hard for you because it brings up one of the Core Wounds - abandonment, abuse, or separation from source. Maybe you asked yourself, 'Where was God when I was hurt? Where was God when this happened?' We've been told we were kicked out of the garden; that women were evil, that humans are evil and we must suffer and toil. Maybe there is some anger there."

And as she spoke, it hit the truth deep in my soul. Tears started to flow. I did feel abandoned, alone, and disconnected. I was angry, hurt, and felt I was not good enough. I felt weak, and that life was only suffering. I understand that this is a core wound and something I will continue to work on. A core wound is one that we share collectively, for generations. You may hear people talk about a need for ancestral healing or cultural healing. This is because of these core wounds. They are bigger than us. They can be an entire nation's trauma, and so they are hard to heal. But that doesn't mean we can't start the process.

Since then, I've spent a lot of time grieving and healing these wounds, and have started to come into a place of love and forgiveness. It is a process, but I think one that is of benefit for all of us. It's in our collective grief and tears, our collective forgiveness and release of this anger, that we will heal this wound and come to a place of love. Together, we will become whole again.

\* \* \*

## Beginner's Mind

Can you come into that place where you don't already have the answer? Where you can feel the curiosity and wonderment you felt as a small child? When you would look for answers in the trees and the sky? This is the beginner's mind. It's why we must go on this journey of self-discovery before we come up with our plan of action.

It's what I always practice when I have a healing session with someone. If I "think" I know what they need before they even walk in the door, then I will surely be wrong! In an energy healing session, I always ask Spirit to "show me" how I can be of service, rather than use my ego to decide. It's turning off the mind and allowing ourselves to be receptive to our intuition and the Universe speaking to us. It's a place of humility, acknowledging we don't have all the answers and can learn from the world around us. It's a beautiful place to exist, because instead of feeling the need to be in control of everything, you can be in the flow of the Universe, floating in the river of life without feeling the need to steer.

\* \* \*

## Living Congruently

Are you living in congruence with your higher purpose, with your heart's desire? This is why we are doing all this work, to discover our higher purpose and heart's desire, so that our actions can be congruent with them. We cannot be hypocrites, though it is so easy to be so. We cannot say "I care about sustainability. I care about the environment and the planet," but continue to do things that are in direct harm to it.

Yes, we make excuses, like the government doesn't give us enough subsidies to pay for our home upgrades or that the companies make everything in plastic, so we can't help that plastic is everywhere. I made lots of excuses myself as an architect. I wanted buildings to be net-zero energy usage, but my employer wouldn't support this financially. So, what could I do? I would tell myself it's not my fault that I can't practice what I believe in. That the world is just too big and I am too small. Does this sound familiar?

It's harder than you think to live congruently! There seems to be something that blocks our way at every turn. But it's still something we must try to do. If we are not in congruence with ourselves, we are in disharmony. And disharmony, internal conflict, is the cause of so many physical and emotional ailments. It causes much of our world's ailments as well. So we must try to live congruently.

Maybe start small. Start with one small thing that you believe in and will act on. Think of something where you say "I know I shouldn't, but..." And then see if you can. Maybe it's a habit of telling little white lies instead of being truthful with a friend or coworker. Maybe it's finally incorporating some vegetarian days into your meal plan. Or standing up for your ideals at work, or following your passion and starting a business instead of waiting for someone else to do so. Take a stand for yourself to come into congruence with your core values. See how it feels. Try it again. And again. And again.

All of these practices can help us come into alignment with our soul and our Spirit. Then we can come into alignment with the Spirit that is outside of us. They will put us on that soul's journey of the hummingbird, and we can fly to a place of Ayni – of love, balance, and harmony.

\* \* \*

# The Way of the Eagle

The Practices of Eagle/Condor help us continue on this deeper journey, finding our relationship with the Universe.

## Indigenous Alchemy

By definition, alchemy means "transforming" and indigenous means "that which is native and naturally occurring." Indigenous alchemy is a process where you can let go of the ideas you identify with, transform the ideas that differentiate you from others by integrating them, and then transcend even those ideas. It is the process of letting go of all that is "you" and transcending into the higher place of Eagle. It is a lot to wrap the head around, but maybe this practice will help.

\* \* \*

## Practice: Identify, Differentiate, Integrate, Transcend

On a piece of paper, or in the book, divide the page into four sections. In the first section, write Identify, the second write Differentiate, the third write Integrate, and the fourth write Transcend. Now, write down all the things about you that you identify with. It could be personality aspects, like "I'm a team player," "I'm a listener," or "I'm a salesperson."

Now, in the next category, write down the qualities you differentiate yourself from. These are things you think to yourself "No, I am definitely NOT these things." It could be you differentiate yourself from people who are snobby and condescending. Or pushy people, or people that are pushovers. Whatever it is, just write it down.

In the third category write things that you would like to integrate into you. These are things you are struggling with accepting into your being. When I did this practice I wrote down loving my body, accepting I am a whole and healed person, and that I am becoming a shaman. The more authentic your answers are, the more self-discovery you will make.

In the last category write down the things that you have transcended. These are things that you used to identify with but no longer define you. An example would be if you raised your children and have now released the mother or father role. Or if you're retired and have let go of your work identity.

Identify

1.
2.
3.
4.

Differentiate

1.
2.
3.
4.

Integrate

1.
2.
3.
4.

Transcend

1.
2.
3.
4.

Now, look at each column. Imagine what it would feel like if you could let go of all the ideas you identify with. Imagine you no longer identify with them, and instead differentiate between the inner "you" and all of these roles or qualities. Just imagine it. As an example, if you wrote down "I'm a team player," imagine what it would feel like if you didn't have a sense of pride or identity in that role, but it was just a "thing" like any other thing. Imagine you had no more ownership of that than of brushing your teeth every day.

Now, imagine what it would feel like if you could take those things that you despise, that you differentiate yourself from, and reconcile yourself with them. Ask yourself, do I differentiate myself from these because secretly there's a small part of me that once identified with them? Like if you differentiate with someone who is snobby, is that because there's a small shadow of a snob still inside of you?

This takes some imagination because we've usually pushed these parts of us into our subconscious. But usually, the things that we are triggered by are pieces of us that we have not yet fully reconciled. Imagine if you could accept and integrate that piece within you to be able to transcend it entirely.

Now, look at the pieces that you are working to integrate. Imagine what it would feel like to fully integrate those and then transcend them entirely. In my example, I could imagine what it feels like to completely love my body and accept it as it is. That I could transcend that entirely and just come into a place of loving acceptance, where it's not even a thing anymore. Even if it is still in my imagination, it's a start for making it a reality.

The last category of transcend is to give us a perspective, to see what it feels like to have transcended a role. If you have transcended the role of 'daughter' because your parents are now gone, can you completely release that role to the universe? Imagine giving all of those things to the Universe, and in that release you are coming closer to that moment when you lose all sense of 'I'-ness and come into complete connection with Spirit.

\* \* \*

## Owning our Projections

I will go into this in more depth in the next chapter, but the idea is that everything that we perceive is just a projection of our psyche. When we see someone that makes us angry, it's an element within ourselves that we haven't come to terms with.

The eagle comes to teach us that reality is entirely within the eye of the beholder. If you see a world of nightmares, maybe it's time for you to heal the nightmares within you. If you see a world of joy and love, then it's because you are reflecting that joy and love within you into the outside world.

The Toltec Shamans believe that the entire world is a dream. That there is the collective dream of humanity and the dream that each of us is in. Because it's all a dream, we can change it, just as we can change our dreams when we are asleep. We just have to wake up, see that it's a dream, and then begin to create a world of harmony and peace, instead a world of nightmares and violence.

* * *

## No Mind

This takes us one step further than the beginner's mind. This is the complete sublimation of the Ego. This is losing all "I" -ness, where your individuality dissolves and you become one with everything. When you can truly come to that place of 'no mind' then you are filled with the wisdom of the Universe. That guides you in your actions, though in this place there aren't actually any actions. Just 'being' is an action in itself.

I can't lead you to that place in this short book, though I wish I could.

However, I hope in sharing my own experiences and meditations, I can inspire you that it's possible. When we transcend our individuality, we see the world from a higher perspective. We can see that world of Ayni and can begin to manifest it in our every day.

\* \* \*

## Mastery of Time

The shamans see time differently. In western cultures, we see time as linear. A shaman sees time as circular, or like a Möbius strip, where the past and future fold back on themselves into the present. A shaman can step outside of ordinary time and track to the past and the future. They can look into the future, tracking all possible destinies. With skill, they can pull a destiny, one that may be unlikely but is possible, and install that into the present, altering our trajectory. This last teaching of Eagle is to show that time is malleable, and we can heal things in both the past and the future. We can heal our ancestor's wounds as we heal our own, and we can also affect future generations by what we do today.

The Q'ero shamans of Peru have looked into the collective future of the planet, and though we are in a time of great upheaval, they have given us hope. They have announced that this time of upheaval is coming to an end, and now is our opportunity to create a world that is in Ayni, that is in harmony and balance. We as humans can evolve into the next version of ourselves, leaving the old ways of violence and discord behind us. The shamans have pulled that destiny into our present, creating a path for us to walk on should we choose to walk it.

The Q'ero Shamans believe this is the time of the Pachacuti, a time when the world is in the process of turning over again. It happens every 500 years, and the last time was when the Spanish came and destroyed the Inca way of life. Now it's time to change again, to let go of the yoke of colonialism and come back into balance with nature. The shamans of the Americas have a prophecy that the Eagle of the North and the Condor of the South will fly together again and the world will be guided by love and compassion. This is my dream of Ayni.

These shamans are sharing their practices with the West, traveling from their mountains in the hope that we answer their call. I have heard that call of Spirit and am accepting the call to service. I am doing my small part to help create this world guided by love, balance, and harmony.

We can also use this time of great change to transform our own wounds and brokenness so we can come back into touch with Spirit. When we are in right relationship with Spirit, we can be in right relationship with our family, friends, and ancestors. Then, as one humanity, we can step into a place of love and compassion, of balance and harmony, and begin to live in Ayni.

\* \* \*

# 10

# The Mirror

*"We but mirror the world. All the tendencies present in the outer world are to be found in the world of our body. If we could change ourselves, the tendencies in the world would also change. As a man changes his own nature, so does the attitude of the world change towards him."*
  *– Mahatma Gandhi*

## Seeing Ourselves in Others

The last few chapters I've talked about healing our own wounds and coming into a loving place with ourselves. Now I want to explore how this can lead to loving relationships with others.

One of the biggest challenges in coming to right relationship with each other is the story of divisiveness and conflict so prevalent in our world right now. Republican vs Democrat, Liberal vs Conservative, West vs. East, Capitalism vs. Communism, the lines have all been drawn. We are in a battle to see whose ideology can defeat the others, with the outcome supposedly being we will all agree on something.

I honestly don't know what the intended outcome is. It doesn't seem to be about agreeing on anything, just to prove the other side "wrong." I find this mindset one of the hardest to overcome because each side believes it is right and is not particularly interested in conversation beyond proving its point. The other side must come over to their way of thinking. If they don't they are inferior, and no longer worth their attention. And since both sides of the argument think the same, no group will ever win or admit they are wrong. Any positive ideas that could actually improve the world get lost in the power struggle.

So how can we break through this gridlock?

The yoga teachings of service, love, and giving will work great in theory, but unfortunately there's so much hate and divisiveness that for the most part people only want to help the people that are already in their camp. Or they want to help from an egoistic stance because it makes them feel better about themselves. We are stuck in an Us vs. Them mentality and only want to help the people in the 'Us' camp. But if we fly up to the place of eagle, we will see there is no Us or Them. We are all energy. We are all connected. The division that we see is created in each of our minds. It is our perspective that needs to shift, not other people.

I truly believe in my heart of hearts, that if we want to move past divisiveness and conflict to a place of balance and harmony, we first have to deal with some of the demons we have lurking inside of ourselves. The ones that make us feel the need to "win" the conflict in the first place. The ones that give us the self-important need to be right at all costs and close our ears from listening to a person with a different view.

That is why I spent so much time talking about facing our own fears and coming to a place of love and self-acceptance. This is how we can begin to own our projections. We can begin to see that all the conflict in the outside world is just a mirror of the conflict in our souls.

The shamans and sages teach that everything we see outside of us is a projection of what is happening inside. The things we differentiate from are also shadows that lie within us.

If we heal the internal conflict, we won't feel the need to engage in winning the external conflict. We could come to a place of listening, compassion, and understanding. We can be the nurturing aspects of the feminine to our neighbors and our adversaries. Or we can step into the wise protective aspect of the masculine, helping those in need. We can find the common language of love that is universal to all cultures and build a community not dependent on being right or wrong.

Mother Teresa once explained to a journalist why she was called to her life of service. She said, "I realized a long time ago that I had a Hitler within me." When we acknowledge we all have our own inner Hitler we can begin to heal ourselves and our interactions with the world.

Carl Jung, the famous Swiss psychologist, would have called this shadow work. He believed that what we see in others, the things we loved or hated, were shadows in ourselves that we had isolated and repressed. If there's a person we see as a tyrant and are disgusted being around, that may be triggering something inside of us that has been repressed, our own inner tyrant. Likewise, if we see someone we admire, maybe someone who is well-spoken and powerful, that is also a part of us that has been repressed. We have that well-spoken and powerful aspect inside, but for some reason didn't feel we could embody it. Maybe we didn't feel safe and supported to let it out, so we repressed those qualities, making us smaller in the process. All of these qualities are our shadows. And working on those shadows is also key to working on our relationship with others.

I like to think of it as a mirror. When I feel anger, hate, or jealousy toward another person, it's really a part of me reflecting back to me. For some reason, I was afraid of that part, and so I stuffed it deep down into my subconscious. Now it's part of my shadow side. Most of us are afraid of exploring this shadow side, afraid of what we might find, but the transformation of those demons into allies can be the most amazing work we can do. If we own our projections, then we truly realize that what happens in the outside world does not dictate our inside world. We can find happiness within, and then project that to the world, just like Gandhi's quote at the beginning of this chapter.

The conflicts we experience with others are our most tremendous opportunities to find the gems that live deep within us. Looking into the mirror and incorporating your shadows can help you come into harmony, balance, and love.

It is said we can never change anyone else, we can only change ourselves. If we are brave enough to heal our shadows, we can become healed and radiant humans. This could inspire others to do it themselves, but it's not the reason we are doing it. We are doing it to be happy, to be free, and to be the fullest and highest version of ourselves.

When we accept that we can't change others, only ourselves, as a basic truth, we don't feel obligated to convince someone else of our ideology. We will embody it, and that will be enough for us. What they choose to believe will be up to them.

Are you ready? If so, let's take a journey into the mirror world.

\* \* \*

## Practice: The Mirror

Journaling Exercise: First, write down the people that really make you angry. They could be people you know personally, political figures, or famous people. Now next to each name, write down the characteristics about that person that really upsets you.

Now, write down the names of people you look up to or admire. Write down their qualities and characteristics, the traits they have that you wished you could have in your life.

Who makes you really angry, and why?

1.
2.
3.
4.

Who do you admire, and why?

1.
2.
3.
4.

Now, look at both lists. What would you say if I told you that you have all of these qualities within you already? That those things that upset you are your own demons you keep tightly under wraps. Imagine what it might be like if you turned those demons into friends and allies. Imagine what they could teach you about yourself, and also what others are feeling when they act that way. Now, think about those things that you admire in others. Imagine that you already have those qualities, but somewhere along the road, you lost the ability to express them. What would it feel like if you could find the courage to embody all those things you admire in others in your own life?

When I did this practice, the qualities I hated most were people who were dismissive, arrogant, self-serving, and fake. Those I valued highly were people who were caring, built community, steadfast in their convictions, and who helped others.

So did that mean that I also contained arrogance, cruelness, dismissiveness, and selfishness? You ask all my friends, and I think they'd say no, that I was a nice, kind, and caring person. But if you asked my husband, the one who knows me better than anyone else, he might say if he was being honest, "Well, yes, she is all that, but sometimes, yeah, she can be pretty mean." They say we can be the cruelest to the ones we love the most.

* * *

## My Mirror

I am eternally grateful that I have found such an equal partner in my husband. He has given me a great opportunity to be my mirror, and to help me in my shadow work. We've been together for 20 years, and still have a tendency to blow our tops at each other. We are both stubborn, sensitive, and opinionated. We both have insecurities from our childhoods and struggle with feeling seen and heard. So sometimes when we feel our side isn't being heard, we just scream a little louder each go around to make sure we get our message across. When we are in a grounded and compassionate place, we can listen and understand what each other is going through, but when our inner demons are triggered, we can explode.

Earlier I talked about the practice of non-engagement and how when I first came into that practice I did so in a very superior way. I was like, well when he starts screaming I just won't engage. I will just say this fight is not worth my energy, and stay away from it. I am a detached observer, amazing, and enlightened, blah blah blah. Well, that worked for a few weeks.

I was still getting angry. I just wasn't acting on it. I hadn't done a thing about dealing with my shadows, just pushed them even further down. To move to a place of non-engagement, and to own my own projections, I had to actually work on that anger. I had to own my projections, and what I was bringing to the argument. But how? I knew it was there, but I didn't know how to move past it. It was a few months later, as I was trying to build my relationship with the divine feminine that I was able to finally see the shadow for what it was and begin to integrate it.

That I was working on my relationship with the divine feminine is no big surprise. There's a recurring story in our patriarchal society that the feminine is less than the masculine. And so women are less than men. That story has been told to us for so many generations, I think very few of us have a good relationship with our feminine side. There is a big push to shift this paradigm and to bring the feminine back into balance. Of course, this is hard for lots of reasons. We have very few roadmaps to do so, as we have effectively wiped out all the feminine or Earth-based cultures that had this balance.

As I was struggling with this idea, I had the opportunity to attend a workshop with the author of several books on the divine feminine, HeatherAsh Amara. Her talk gave me great insight into why I was struggling, and also gave me a path forward. Not just in the struggles with my divine feminine, but also in how the fights with my husband were tied to that struggle.

She said there is tremendous fear in our collective psyche about women coming into our own power. Women were murdered en masse for being different, bold, or powerful. They were called witches, whores, and heathens, but their only crime was trying to live in their power. This core wounding and fear for our survival is part of our collective shadow. I knew it was part of my shadow. All the things that triggered me were so deeply related to this - feeling powerless, not heard, not respected. Even the big struggle I had with the shamanic teaching of "keeping a secret" was related. Deep inside, I felt flawed and broken. I felt I'd never be able to come into a place of proud, feminine, loving power.

In the workshop, Ms. Amara suggested that when we see a wounding or vulnerability inside us, we have to give it love and space in our lives so it can share its message. We shouldn't be angry with it or feel ashamed. It is a great wounding not of our own doing. We would not be angry at our arm if it had a cut on it, instead we would ask ourselves how we can heal it. Instead of anger or shame, she suggested we approach it with curiosity and love. Ask it what needs to be grieved, what needs to be healed, and what needs to be loved. The longer we disown these shadows, these demons, these mirror projections, the longer our soul will stay split.

A few days later, I drew the Sorcerer card in my oracle card deck. The Sorcerer card is an opportunity for us to transmute the darkness within, but most of us would be tempted to return it to the deck and draw another card. We say to ourselves, "Oh surely not, I am not a sorcerer! I am full of love and light and goodness. This must be a card for another person." However, this time I knew it was synchronicity. I was ready to face my shadows. I went on a meditation journey into the underworld, to see what gems I could uncover in the depths of my soul. Here is my journey.

\* \* \*

*I call upon my jaguar. She comes to my side, and with her eyes for guidance, we go into the deep darkness of the jungle. In the darkness I feel anger, resentment, and jealousy. I'm jealous that my husband finds success in the* corporate world where I have only found roadblocks. I'm angry and resentful that my passion for practicing sustainable architecture and designing for people in need has been belittled and dismissed in my job, while his has been celebrated. I'm angry that we as women have been disenfranchised. I'm angry that we have been repressed. My ego jumps up and down, wanting power, wanting revenge, wanting to show just how strong I can be.

But jaguar tells me nature doesn't hold anger. If I look to nature as my guide for finding balance, how can I hold on to this anger? Nature acts for survival, family, and protection, not for anger or revenge. I ask Spirit how I can transmute this anger. I know that if I step into my power from this place of anger and darkness, it will poison all my actions. I will only further the patriarchy. I give the anger my acknowledgment. I let that anger fill me up, righteous anger, anger from so many generations. It fills me up, red hot and full of rage, until it bursts into flame. And the flames burn and turn to ash. I call on the rain, asking it to soothe my burnt body.

As the rain falls, it extinguishes the flames and I feel each drop is a tear for the loss of so much happiness. The water fills the space all around me, so many tears, until I am floating in an ocean. An ocean of tears and grief. As I float in this ocean, a dolphin swims up to me, telling me to play. It shows me how to find joy again, to live in the present. She says to me with her eyes, "What happened before is done, and what will happen tomorrow, who can say? There is only now."

The resentment falls away, and I dive down with her. Deep, deep into the ocean, to the bottom of the sea, and then even deeper. I go deep into the Earth, with the tree roots and the fungi and microorganisms. And here in this space, I lose all sense of time. What is now, what is tomorrow. In this feeling of timelessness there is no space for anger or joy, only stillness.

I sit with the stillness for a moment, and then I am pulled up into the sky, by the wings of many birds. They carry me higher and higher, until I see a rainbow. And as I look at that rainbow I feel called to a place of forgiveness. Forgiving those who created the nightmare that hurt so many, and forgiving

111

*myself for living in such a small way. Spirit forgives us, for we didn't know what we were doing. But now I know. Now I understand. And so, I must fill myself up with this dream, with the rainbow, with the joy and the flowers. I must fill myself up with love and timelessness. I must let go of the competition of who is right and who is wrong, who will win and who will lose, and just come into the now. Nature is love, and so am I.*

\* \* \*

I share this journey for a few reasons, first to inspire, and second to show how we don't do these things alone.

Getting to know our shadow side is terrifying for most of us. Why else would our society have filled itself with so many avoidance mechanisms? I teach yoga relaxation and have many friends who say they love the experience when they come, but struggle to find time to make it a regular practice. Why is that? Why do we fill our days and lives with busy? I think it's because we are taught that's what a successful life is, but also because we are afraid of stillness. We are afraid of what might speak to us in the quiet moments. We are afraid of ourselves.

And so, I share my journey, because while it started off with fear and anger, the journey was full of beauty and love. This is what happens when we make friends with our shadows. This is what happens when we look in the mirror with love, not judgment. We can realize that we are not a monster and that we are worthy of love. And if we heal those demons with love and compassion we can blossom into the most beautiful flower.

The other thing to note is that we are not alone in this journey. Notice that when I decided to go on this shamanic journey I first called on my jaguar. She is my power animal that takes me into my scary places. If you have a relationship with a power animal, an angel, or a spirit guide, call on that entity to help you. If you are religious, send out a prayer.

And as the journey continued, other things showed up to help me in my process. The dolphin, who has been a spirit animal companion for many years, came to show me the way back to joy. The birds came to lift me into the sky. All the elements of nature came to help me transmute my anger. The fire, water, earth, and air. While I didn't call on them specifically, they each came. Mother Nature, Pachamama, is here to help us in our healing journey. If you are ever feeling overwhelmed, take a trip out to nature. She will hold you in her loving embrace, and guide you to a place of peace and love. Call in the four elements, and welcome their wisdom into your life.

And don't forget Carl Jung, who coined the term shadow work, was a psychologist. Look to a trusted psychologist, therapist, or religious or spiritual leader, to help you on this journey. Just know that you are not alone. If you are sincere in your desire to go on a journey to uncover these secrets, ask the Universe to help you find your guides. The Universe is miraculous in how it will put an opportunity out there for you.

Looking into the mirror is worth it, every time.

First, it will help you to love yourself, and to love yourself is the greatest gift.

Also, when we realize that what triggers us are our shadows, we realize it's the same for other people. When we understand what other people are doing is because of their shadows, their stuff, we can stop taking it so personally. It isn't about us, it's about their own pain and heartbreak. I mean sure, we'll always get upset, offended, or frustrated by another person, but we can stop thinking their actions are about us. We may even wonder what happened in their lives that made them so angry or frustrated, as we uncovered the same things in our own lives.

Were they abandoned or betrayed? Do they feel lonely and unloved? And if we can realize this, we can look at their actions with a little more compassion, just as we start to look at our faults and flaws with compassion.

But maybe the most important thing about looking into the mirror is forgiveness.

We are all a little bit broken. Truthfully, we are all a lot bit broken. We all have shadow sides. We all have aspects that are hurtful to ourselves and each other. We all have anger and violence in us as much as we have kindness and compassion. And as long as we hate that part of us that is also in others we will stay a broken world.

Can we find forgiveness in our hearts? Can we forgive ourselves? That we are not the perfect mother, father, spouse, daughter, or friend? Can we find forgiveness for our loved ones? That they also are broken in their own ways, just doing the best they can. Can we forgive strangers or even our enemies? To know that each one of them has this whole shadow side too? That they also find kind of scary, and maybe a little intimidating.

If we plant a garden, we may have 10 tomato plants. They all came from the same seeds, but some are tall, some are short, some are diseased, and some are healthy. Though they all came from the same seeds, there were so many different factors that affected their growth. Not enough sun, too much sun, too much water, too little water, aphids or tomato worms invading, or weeds choking them out. We don't judge the plant for the things that it can't control, but as gardeners we will do our best to give that plant its best opportunity.

We are all human plants, all of us. We all have in our DNA the blueprint to be a shining radiant luminous human. But then, stuff happened. It could have even been before we were born. Maybe our parents didn't know if they could afford us, or we were a product of abuse. Maybe we were born into a poor household with limited opportunity, or we were born into a rich household that had all the opportunity but no love. There are so many factors that shaped us as we grew. Yes, some of them are in our control, but truly so many are not. We judge ourselves and each other for these things that are out of our control. We feel shame, for ourselves and for others, instead of nurturing and growing the things that are in our control.

Let us all make a promise to ourselves. Let's stop judging ourselves and each other for the things that are outside of our control and instead work on feeding our souls and our bodies with love and kindness so that we can grow into better humans. Then our garden will be strong and full of love and abundance.

\* \* \*

AYNI

* * *

# 11

# Learning from Nature

*"Nature is our best teacher."*
*- Unknown*

Just as my jaguar told me that anger and revenge don't live in nature, nature can offer so many other lessons about ourselves and our place in the world. Nature really can be our best teacher, and I think that so much of our suffering today is because we've lost that connection with her. We've lost our ability to listen.

## The Feathers

Through those random acts of synchronicity, I was gifted four feathers to assist in my shamanic healings. In many cultures, feathers are sacred connections to both Spirit and to the animal that offered up the feather. My feathers are from a hawk, a snow goose, a pheasant, and a black vulture. I've used them in my healings, but one day Spirit asked me to really connect with each of them, to ask them for their story. This is the message they shared, and I believe it is one all of us can learn from.

117

\* \* \*

*The Hawk:*

*She soars in the sky, high above the fray. She looks for food, to feed herself, and to feed her children. She is strong and perfect in her predator nature. It is not an easy path to be a predator. It is often lonely and solitary. She does not always find food and spends many nights hungry. Hers is a cycle of feast and famine. But it is who she is, and she is perfect in this manifestation. She sits atop the tallest tree, watching, patiently waiting for just the right moment. She conserves her energy, using an air thermal to glide effortlessly on the wind, [c1] or sitting patiently on a tree, waiting for the moment to act.*

*The Snow Goose:*

*He is community. His flock flies great distances as brothers and sisters. They share the work, flying in Vs high in the atmosphere where the air is thin. They migrate to the food sources, and food is bountiful. They protect themselves by traveling in great numbers, knowing that not everyone will make it, but that the species will thrive. He is part of a collective, where the group's needs outweigh the individual's. The community is more important.*

*The Pheasant:*

*The beautiful feather of a rooster pheasant is beauty for beauty's sake. Not everything in nature must have a purpose or function. Life is beautiful, just because. Maybe there is some evolutionary story to the beauty of his feathers, but that's not all of the story. A feather can shimmer in the sunshine and dance in the breeze for sheer joy and celebration of life. We must embrace beauty.*

*The Vulture:*

*She tells me all in life is as it is meant to be. Nothing is wasted, nothing is*

118

*amiss. What dies becomes life again; what is born must die. Life and death are a cycle, and every organism in nature is part of this cycle. Everything and every action in nature are perfect and organic. All of us play our part, there is no good or bad. Don't judge what you don't understand, for it to plays a part in the circle of life.*

\* \* \*

Each feather and each animal are so different, and yet essential to each other. The predator, the prey, and the scavenger, all need each other to exist and complete the cycle. Without the predators, the geese would become overpopulated and starve. Without the scavengers, we would have disease and more death. And the pheasant is a beautiful reminder that nature is not just about survival, it is also about beauty.

As humans, we are unique and complex beings. We are both predators and beings that thrive on community. We live off the land and also kill. We contain great capacity for beauty and love as well as death and destruction. We are part of the cycle of death and rebirth even if we don't acknowledge it. I believe the messages from the feathers were to remind us that we must acknowledge and respect all of these aspects within ourselves and each other.

Let's look at this from the aspect of masculine and feminine natures. I don't mean gender, but the idea we have both qualities within us, the strong masculine and the nurturing feminine. Coming into balance with them will allow us to become fully embodied as a human. If the hawk represents the masculine force of predator and strength, the goose could represent the feminine nature of community, nurturing, and personal sacrifice for a higher purpose.

Our society has spent an awful lot of energy pushing the hawk mindset. Especially in the Western world, the qualities of the hawk are what is rewarded. The strength for sure, taking what you need in life to feed your family, but also the loneliness and isolation. The feeling of competition for limited resources resonates very strongly with the hawk. They will fight over territory because they know that an acre of land can only support so many birds of prey. Predators embody how humans interact with each other right now.

But in humans, this is one-sided and on its own is not in balance. Why? Because this is not our entire nature. We are also the snow goose, we are community and working together. Our nature also includes beauty, we yearn for it in art and song. We express ourselves through our plumage, and our decoration, and there's nothing wrong with this. It's part of who we all are as humans. We are also death and rebirth. Death and destruction are needed for growth and life. We cannot just grow and grow and grow; it's out of balance. The vulture reminds us of that. It reminds us nothing is permanent, and that all things that live must die, and all that die will be reborn in a new way.

The patriarchy of today has pushed the mindset of the hawk so effectively, that we look at the goose as weaker. Even the concept of communism, which was supposed to be about community, is expressed as dictatorships in our modern society. It still pushes the hawk mindset. Why would we want to put others in front of our own needs? That won't help us at all. We will lose ground, lose resources, become weak, and the next thing you know some other government or tribe will come in and destroy us.

But the snow goose is not weaker, one could maybe argue it is stronger! Geese migrate to wherever the food is, so they never go hungry. They raise their children in great communities, where they are protected and ensure survival. They are resilient and resourceful in sharing the work, by flying together. They have safety in numbers, and their numbers are exploding. The snow geese populations have increased from 1 million birds in the 1960s to 3 million birds today. In many states, hunters are encouraged to shoot as many as can because they're decimating their Arctic habitat. This is, of course, due to the lack of predators from climate change, as well as changes in agricultural practices. But see how strong the feminine aspects of community and partnership can be. How resilient and powerful are the qualities of coming together and putting others' needs in front of our own?

The snow goose community reminds me of Ayni, of mutualism and reciprocity. If I give today, then I know tomorrow I will get what I need. You see a group of geese land on a pond. Of course, they squabble and complain to no end, but they are family. They are community. They share their resources and protect each other.

The hawk teaches us that life is hard and that we must be alert and on guard. It teaches us to be strong and decisive. The hawk shows us that there are cycles of feast and famine but to not give up hope, because we must get through these to survive. But the goose reminds us that we do not have to be alone in these struggles. We can find community, support, and love with each other. Solving problems alone is not the only way, and love and community can make us stronger, not weaker.

The pheasant teaches us we can find beauty in all of life. We can celebrate that some of us have blue eyes and some of us have brown. We can celebrate that some of us glitter and shine for no reason at all, and some of us are more practical and pragmatic. The pheasant rooster is full of pomp and circumstance, and the hen keeps herself hidden so her babies can be safe. Nature teaches us that both are perfectly okay. Do not judge the rooster because you are a hen. Do not judge the hen, because you are a rooster. Neither is good or bad. They just are.

And the vulture asks why we are so afraid of death, because it is part of life, too. The one thing that is certain in life is that it will eventually end. So why do we have so much fear around death? Death and life are all part of the circle. If our fear of death paints how we interact in life, it diminishes the joy that we could feel. Instead of running toward life, we are running away from death. We run away from heartbreak, instead of running toward love. We run away from community, because we are afraid of rejection, and yet in that fear of rejection we end up being isolated and alone.

We yearn for balance and harmony, and nature shows us the way. To have balance we need all of these things, within us and in the world. If all of humanity were to become hawks, the world would be out of balance. Likewise, if we were all geese, we wouldn't have the strength and resiliency of the hawk. Without the beauty in life as shown to us by the pheasant, there'd be no balance either. We need art and music to live a full and enriched life. And without death, the vulture teaches us, there can be no life.

Nature offers us this wisdom. To help us understand the world, and also to understand ourselves. She invites us to take the messages of all the feathers into our own hearts and relationships. Humans are so special. We can be both-and, and not either-or. How will we choose to live?

* * *

# 12

# Coming Together

*"I believe a leaf of grass is no less than the journeywork of the stars."*
– Walt Whitman

## Building Community

Community. Or in the Quechua language, the language of the Andes, they use the word Ayllu (Ay-you): Ayllu means community, but the word is bigger than the basic idea of community in the English language. It includes all of the beings in a community- the humans, the animals, the plants, and the natural elements. It also acknowledges the ancestors and the future generations as part of the community, and that all of these parts are interconnected.

You could say ayllu means family but in a broader sense. It is the extended family of a community, a village, the people you encounter in your daily life, the animals in your community, your ancestors, and the future generations. It's a beautiful word because it's all-inclusive, and is based on the fundamental principles of love, balance, harmony, and reciprocity. If you bring those ideas into your community, your community becomes so much more than just your neighbors, co-workers, or social media group.

I want to start this chapter by reflecting on the idea of community. What would it look like to come into right relationship with all the people we encounter in our daily life—the good, the bad, and the indifferent? Can we come into a loving, giving, and compassionate relationship with the neighbor across the street who has controversial political signs? Or the checkout person at the grocery store? Or a co-worker that we dislike? It's easy to want to build communities of like-minded people and then shut out anyone else who is different. Our social media algorithms, our suburban segregations, and our governments encourage this behavior. Humans have always been tribalistic, and being in a global economy has not changed this tendency. But to start to heal the world and to live in Ayni, we need to come to the place of One Tribe, One Planet.

In a very simplistic view of history, before the globalization that began in the 20th Century, each country was fairly segregated. Each country had its own cultural identity, its own language, and, in general, was pretty racially homogenous. If there was diversity, it was still often segregated. In the U.S., which has for many years been called the melting pot, populations are still segregated. Of course, much of that was due to oppressive acts of colonialism and forced segregation of the population, but the outcome has still been one of division.

Being different has rarely been encouraged, especially looking different or acting different. We only have to remember back a few years ago that gay and bi-racial marriages were not only frowned upon but illegal in the U.S., and are still illegal in many countries. But as humanity has awoken to the idea of diversity and inclusion, that love is love, and that there is strength in difference, these paradigms are slowly starting to shift. And thank goodness!

Diversity, equity, and inclusion are finally becoming commonplace words in our society. We're coming to terms with the past, with the damage that colonialism and the patriarchy have done to marginalized populations. There are so many ideas and movements around the world to heal this injustice. Books upon books are being written about how we can build a global community and further these ideals. With so many different and beautiful ideas, what can I add to this conversation?

As a middle-aged, privileged, white woman, I don't truly understand what it feels like to have been disenfranchised for generations, though I want to learn. I have not experienced the effects of segregation and racism on my ability to succeed, though I want to help close the gap and heal the wounds. Truly all I can add is my heart's desire to build community, to learn and understand other's perspectives, and to do so with humility. All I can add is my own experience and my journey, and to respect and listen to other's as well.

My heart is calling me to explore the idea of a community that embraces all our gifts and unique differences. It's calling me to start healing our shadows, so we can have relationships with each other based on unconditional love, instead of scarcity and fear. It's asking me to find a way to live in Ayni, with all living things, and so that is the path I walk in this book and in my own life.

Whatever path calls you to find right relationship with each other, I hope they all lead to the same goal—to celebrate our diversity but to also find our commonality. By accepting each other not as we wished we would be, but as we are, right now in this moment. This can lead us to a place of love and compassion.

\* \* \*

# Practice: Creating Sacred Space around the World

I invite you to come to this place of community in your imagination through a short practice of opening sacred space. This practice brings us into connection with the Universe and wraps us in a safe and supportive bubble of love and light. Then we can extend that bubble over our community, our Allyu, and imagine what that might feel like. Then we can send it over the entire planet.

Sit comfortably, in a chair, or on the floor. Feel your feet grounding into the Earth. Even if you are inside, feel the life force of the Earth through the floor, extending up from the soil and into your body. Now feel a connection to the sky through your head. Feel the air, the sun, the wind, all the elements of the sky and the heavens. Feel that you are part of both.

Now bring your hands to your heart in a prayer position. With a deep breath in, pull that Earth energy up from the ground, into your hands, and then bring your hands up over your head reaching to the sky. Then slowly, with intention, exhale your breath and open your arms up wide around you, like you are making a big circle. Starting from above your head, extending that circle to the side and then back down to the floor. Do this one or two more times until you feel the circle of love and light around you. Invite in Spirit and your ancestors, and all the wisdom of the Universe into your circle.

Now, imagine your whole community. Your family, your friends, your neighbors, the people you see occasionally, and even the people you know but don't like much. Bring your hands to your heart and as you lift up into the sky, imagine you are sending that circle of love and light and protection to all of them. Sending them goodwill, peace, and love. Imagine what that feels like, for all of us to be in that beautiful bubble of sacred space. Imagine you are bringing all of those people in your community into that circle.

Now, one more time, bring your hands to your heart, and extend them up to the sky and send that bubble of protection over the entire planet. Send that wish of love and light and support to everyone in the whole world, those suffering from poverty, war, or oppression. Send love and light and the idea of community to all of the animals, the plants, and the stones. And just sit within that space. Feel what it feels like. Does it feel full of love? Is there sadness? What healing is needed there? Just observe, without judgment.

Then, when you are ready, close the circles. Starting with your hands on the ground, close that circle you opened over the entire planet. Move your hands from the ground up to the sky in a big circle, come back to your heart, and then release back to the Earth. Then close the circle over your community. Then finally close that circle over yourself.

*  *  *

A few months ago, I was traveling with a co-worker on a long drive. He's from rural Colorado. Growing up in a conservative and religious household, he lives on acres of land and works in construction and highway maintenance. I grew up on the East Coast with progressive parents, went to a private university, and work in a white-collar office job. We have very different backgrounds, different political views, and different life experiences, but he's always been one of my favorite people. He is just a good person, and very easy to talk to.

We talked back and forth, about work, family, this and that. I asked why there are so many butterflies flying over the road and he said they are attracted to the alfalfa fields this time of year. We talked about climate change, the drought, and how it's changing what crops are grown. We talked about what we were like when we were teenagers, and how much trouble we both used to get into. We talked about raising our kids and how hard it is for them to afford rent or a mortgage right now, or to find a job with decent benefits. After a while, he says to me, "You know, I guess at the end of the day all of us have a whole lot more in common than we have differences. We're all just trying to find happiness and raise our families the best way we know how. Maybe we really aren't all so different after all."

Humans are not solitary beings. Going back to the beginnings of our species, we've always had community. We need each other. At first, it was for survival—for protection or for hunting. And then our community became a part of our identity. We developed a shared language, shared songs, and shared stories. Our community was our village, our safety, and our support network. It was everything.

As the world has become so connected through globalization, ironically, we've also become more isolated. We have blurred the lines of community. What is community? Is it your neighbors that you barely know? Your church group or work group or friend group? Is it the people in your social media feed? Is it people from your same background? Who can you count on when you need something? Who do you turn to when you're feeling alone? Most of us don't live in small villages anymore, and our chosen community can span oceans.

Many groups have recognized this and are trying to find a way to create community in our digital and global world, but one of the side effects of that is to further silo ourselves into groups we align with. Living in a small town or village meant that your community included people you DIDN'T like - the annoying neighbor, the guy with different political views. But you just had to figure out how to get along, for the sake of the village. Living in a village meant that sometimes we had to compromise, to pick our battles, and to smile anyway. Now that we have a global community, we can pick and choose who gets to be in it. When we pick and choose, we don't have to find out our shared interests with people we don't like, we just delete them from our Facebook group, or ghost them from our social circle.

Today, Planet Earth is calling for humanity to be one giant community, for the sake of the planet. It is not asking us to all speak the same language or have the same customs or even to get along perfectly. It is asking us to rediscover that we have more in common than different. That we are all humans, trying our best, wanting to raise our families, have enough food to eat, and to find happiness and contentment in our time here on this planet.

This won't happen by someone else deciding to do something. It won't happen by a government making a rule that we all need to work together. This will only happen by each one of us deciding that it's important. We must be the change that we want to see in the world. If we want to see a world that gets along with each other, we must get along with each other. If we want to see people showing compassion and forgiveness, we must show compassion and forgiveness. There is no "other" anymore, it's only "we."

It's so easy for us to say, "But what I do won't make a difference." But I disagree! It does make a difference. Do not diminish our power so easily. Everything we do makes a difference. Whether we are kind or cruel to a pet makes a difference. Whether we are giving or frugal with our love to a child makes a difference. Whether we say "Hi" to the person at the grocery store or help a person with a door when they are carrying a big package. It all makes a difference.

Each of us is as small as a grain of sand and as mighty as a star. As Walt Whitman said, "A leaf of grass is no less than the journeywork of the stars." I believe this and have created my whole business practice on it. I teach my clients and students that they are already as perfect as the Milky Way or a tall and majestic oak tree, and that they have more power inside them than they realize.

A blade of grass can change its destiny by bending itself to the sun or growing its roots deeper into the Earth. It can send out seeds and, over time, transform the entire landscape. It doesn't ask someone else to do it, it accepts its power, limited as it is, and forges ahead. If we want to see a world where humans live in harmony with each other and the planet, then WE need to be the humans that create that world. We need to send out those seeds.

I am not a Shaman from Peru or a wise and learned Yogi who lived in an ashram since childhood. While I have gone deep into the practices of yoga and shamanism, I am not from a long line of healers, nor have I spent years in the forest learning from the elders. In truth, I am nobody. I'm no greater or more qualified to explore this idea than anyone else. All I have is my experience, my journey, and the love in my heart.

Yet I humbly believe these are the greatest qualifications, because I have found the real truth in life is that any one of us is as powerful as anyone else. That we are all nothing and everything. Just as I have gone on a journey of self-discovery and realization, so can you. You don't need a degree in spirituality or to have been born to a shamanic lineage. You just need a sincere desire to find love and light in your life. I am just a pebble in a sea of pebbles. One human in a planet of eight billion.

But maybe this one pebble can bring love and light to its neighboring pebbles. Then if they do the same, we can transform the entire shoreline and then the entire ocean. And remember, though I am only one pebble, so is everyone else. The people on TV acting self-important, the oligarchs controlling the governments, they too are just one pebble. Just as a polar bear is only one pebble, a blade of grass, or an actual pebble is just a pebble. And if each of us is as important as the other, then it's an illusion that anyone has "power" over us. It may be an illusion some are trying to push, or have put systems in place to enforce, but we do not have to believe it anymore.

\* \* \*

# 13

# Leavers and Takers

*"No one saves us but ourselves. No one can and no one may.*
*We ourselves must walk the path"*
*- Gautama Buddha*

## Moving Past the Patriarchy

When I'd just graduated college 20 or so years ago, a friend gave me a book about a gorilla. That book was called *Ishmael* by Daniel Quinn, and it opened my eyes to a whole new world. This book talked about the leavers and the takers. Humanity used to be leavers. We operated from a basic understanding that we were but one of the many creatures in the world and that we needed to leave enough for others. The agricultural revolution, the industrial revolutions, all these revolutions that supposedly have made our lives better have also made us takers. We take and take, hoping that the next generation will figure out how to replenish things. But deep down we know if we continue to take that soon there will be nothing left.

The gorilla in the book implored us to abandon the practice of being takers and come back to being leavers. For many years, this message sat with me, as it sits with many of us, in a place of helpless frustration. But today, here I am, writing this book, not because I want to share a message of frustration, but because I believe that we have the power to become leavers once again. Tom come back to a balanced relationship with the planet. To come back to Ayni.

Though colonialism tried so hard to eradicate all the leavers, they were not successful. Their message remains, and many of us are now waking up to listen to it.

The Q'ero Shamans came down from their mountains after 500 years in hiding to share their wisdom. They have entrusted this message to many Westerners, like Dr. Alberto Villoldo, tasking them to share and spread their teachings. They teach that now is the time of the Pachacuti, the great turning over of things. Now is the time when we need to come back to Ayni.

Corbin Harney, a Shoshone spiritual leader, made it his life's work to share his "nature way" with others, speaking at the United Nations and conferences worldwide. He taught that nature put all living things here for us to take care of, not to destroy. He spoke for years to all the governments of the world, encouraging them to work with each other to come back into balance with nature.

Finally, at the recent United Nations Summit for Biodiversity, the leaders recognized indigenous wisdom should be brought into the summit. Though indigenous communities make up only 5% of our population they still protect 80% of the world's biodiversity. At the Summit, 497 of the 15,723 people registered to attend represented indigenous nations or organizations. Though none of those indigenous nations had decision-making status, at least there was finally recognition of their wisdom.

Toltec Shaman Don Miguel Ruiz shared the ancient wisdom of the

Toltecs in his famous book "The Four Agreements." He showed us how could begin to wake ourselves up from the collective nightmare and begin to dream a world of love and beauty.

The great Lakota Chief Crazy Horse prophesized near the end of his life, "Upon suffering beyond suffering, the Red Nation shall rise again, and it shall be a blessing for a sick world. A world filled with broken promises, selfishness, and separations. A world longing for light again. I see a time of seven generations when all the colors of mankind will gather under the sacred Tree of Life and the whole Earth will become one circle again. In that day, there will be those among the Lakota who will carry knowledge and understanding of unity among all living things and the young white ones will come to those of my people and ask for this wisdom. I salute the light within your eyes where the whole Universe dwells. For when you are at that center within you and I am that place within me, we shall be one."

\* \* \*

It feels to me that this time is here. The world is longing for light again, and understanding the unity among all living things is the way.

I can't call this a "How-To" Book, because the journey to finding our interconnectedness is not in a book. It is in your own personal relationship with nature and all living things. It's in opening up to listen to the wind and the water and to feel the earth under your feet. It's in coming to a place of love and harmony and then acting from that place. It's in acknowledging the cycles of the planet and becoming a part of them, not separate from them.

First, we must unpack all the stories that we've been holding on to and come into right relationship with ourselves. Then we can come into right relationship with each other. We can begin to hear the world outside of us, we can listen to nature. When we are finally receptive, we can come into right relationship with the world. We can find love, balance, and harmony for ourselves, and for the planet. We can move away from the mentality of the taker because we understand that our collective future must be based on leaving enough for future generations.

When the Europeans colonized America, they told themselves the story of Manifest Destiny, that 'God' had ordained them to be there. They believed it was their "divine right" to subjugate and eliminate all the indigenous peoples, plants, and animals of America, and to spread across the nation. But this was not a divine right, it was a plague. This belief did not recognize the value of nature, or that balance needs to be maintained. It preached that life is a linear progression of never-ending growth.

In nature, organisms that have uncontrolled growth are also called viruses. They are a plague and bring death and destruction in their wake. Like locusts that spread over a grass field, humanity has spread all over the planet, destroying the natural balance. And so to keep the balance, the Earth is responding in the way any organism would to a virus. She sends great storms, droughts, heat waves, and other changes in the climate. This is the fever to knock down the virus.

I think most indigenous peoples would agree that it is not the Earth that is out of balance, its humanity. If you take a walk in the forest, if you sit with the trees, you will feel the balance and harmony is still there, but are we a part of it? It's our separation from our planet and our surroundings that needs to be fixed. Since humanity did it to ourselves, we also must be the ones to fix it.

Many of us were taught we were kicked out of the Garden of Eden. It sometimes feels as if we almost don't have a 'right' to have that deep connection with the Earth. Maybe we were, maybe we weren't. It doesn't matter, because that is the past. The wisdom of the leavers of the world gives us a pathway to come back to the Garden. The indigenous peoples around the planet, the Earth Keepers, were never kicked out of the Garden. They have always listened to the cycles of the Earth and understood that humans were a part of it, not above it. We can look to their wisdom to guide us back home again.

The idea of leavers and takers talked about in Daniel Quinn's book is the same as the idea of Ayni, of giving before receiving, of sacred reciprocity. This idea is what we need most in our broken world right now.

\* \* \*

# AYNI

***

# 14

# Ayni and Munay

*"Happiness is when what you think, what you say, and what you do are in harmony."*
*– Mahatma Gandhi*

When I asked my shaman teacher to write a foreword for this book it was because I hoped that he, more than most, would understand my heart's wish to live in Ayni. He believed in that dream and in wanting to reconnect with our Mother Earth. After he read the draft manuscript, Spirit downloaded to him a new and powerful myth about Ayni, one that asked to be shared. It is the advent of Ayni.

## The Advent of Ayni – by P.J. Sanderson

*The Great Mother took one step back,*
*She saw the earth from space for the first time since her creation was complete,*
*She placed the planet a perfect distance from Grandfather Sun,*
*This sphere of blue and green was pure beauty,*

*Her waters glistened gold in the tender rays of the sun light,*
*'She is almost perfect', thought the Great Mother of her daughter,*
*'I name her Pachamama,'*

*But there was still one thing missing from this Eden,*
*So the Great Mother took a deep intake of breath,*
*And blew the final sacred ingredient upon Pachamama,*
*The universe felt a force like never before,*
*'What is this warm and sacred gift which you have blessed me with, Great Mother,' smiled Pachamama?*

*'Daughter, you have been blessed with the force of Ayni,' said the Great Mother,*
*'She will bring you balance and harmony,*
*One day,*
*Millions of years from now,*
*Your caretakers will lose their way and try to leave your Garden,*
*They will forget how to love you and struggle to keep you alive,*
*A unifying force called Ayni has been woven into your DNA,*
*Books and poems will be written by wise souls,*
*This deep feminine force will be activated,*
*'She will breathe life into all who walk gently upon you,'*
*'She will be your saving grace.'*

*'What is this Ayni you speak of?' asked Pachamama,*
*'It is the greatest hug of all from the Cosmic Mother,' said the Great Mother,*
*'The revealing of the invisible strands of love which interconnect the universe,*
*Ayni is the Great illumination of the cosmos,*
*The gentle whisper of the Great Spirit on the healing eastern wind to those who inhabit you,*

*The joining of 24 billion hands,*
*The intertwining of 12 billion hearts,*
*An unwrapping of peace,*
*A quantum remembering of the mass consciousness,*
*Reconnecting every grain of stardust,*
*Recharging it with the Godforce,*
*She is the healing sound of the heavens,*
*The archangel of white light, unity and community,*
*She is the undiscovered coding which will save the human race,*

*Ayni sees time like the ocean,*
*Some will only see the chaos and the tick tock of the waves,*
*Yet the deeper you go,*
*The slower she flows,*
*The more magnificent your appreciation of her stillness and her order,*
*She is the tuning into your own heartbeat,*
*The feeling into the rhythm of the universal river,*
*Ayni is the silence in the thunder,*
*The love of the mother,*
*She is the glimpse of the world through the eyes of the Great Spirits heart,*
*The dissolving of war, pain and destruction,*
*The building of bridges, community and pure love,*
*She is the unburying of beauty,*
*She is the secret work which has been done within you.*
*The place in the soul where neither time nor space can touch,*
*The bridge to a new destiny for earthkind.*
*A time before time,*
*A space before space,*
*She has returned,*
*And she is here to stay.*

# Mutualism and Love

So Dear Readers, what do you think of this idea of Ayni? I invite you to let these words sink in. To feel them in your heart and soul. To imagine this world of Ayni.

In many ways, Ayni is the opposite of how much of our society runs at the moment. The Western world of colonialism and patriarchy teaches us the world is a place of fear and scarcity. That it's every man for themselves, and we must fight to control limited resources. The American Dream was based on the idea of rugged individualism, but also of competition and conquest. That dream was that mankind is here to tame nature and accumulate wealth. Colonialism taught that humanity is above nature, and even above other humans. If you are mightier in Strength, you must be mightier in Spirit.

This dynamic, while it worked for the chosen few for a few thousand years, is cracking at the seams. Colonialism's basic story is that the world is for a chosen few and, if you're not one of them, then get out of the way. Its second story is that if you work hard enough, and fall into line, then maybe, just maybe, you'll get accepted into the club. But this is a story, invented by people who love power and want to control and oppress others. Entry to the club is limited to those chosen few, and they are destroying the planet.

This story doesn't have to be our reality, it's just a story. A story based on F.E.A.R., False Evidence Appearing Real. There can be another way to live.

The people of the Andes lived in a different way. The Inca, and even before the Inca, lived by five basic principles. The first four are living in munay (right heart), yachay (right thought), ilankay (right doing), and kawsay (living life in harmony). The fifth is Ayni – reciprocity and mutualism. Ayni is the backbone, the framework for all the other principles.

Why do we need right heart, right thought, and right doing to live life in harmony and reciprocity? Because most of us have been living in the world of scarcity and fear for so long we don't even remember what it feels like to act from our hearts. We've been conditioned that our actions should be about making money, accumulating things, and gaining status. So any actions we make, well-intentioned or not, come from a conditional or transactional mindset. We may think "I will volunteer at this organization," but inside we say to ourselves, "but they better appreciate me and say thank you and how kind I am for being here." To come into Ayni we must act from a place of giving, not from a place of receiving accolades or appreciation. Our actions must be in harmony and for the betterment of all living things. To do that, we must act from the heart.

Munay means love, but more than the English word for love. It is the big unconditional and transcendental love for everyone and everything. It is love for yourself and for all that is around you, like the love described in the poem from the Cosmic Mother. Mother Nature/God/Spirit feels munay for all of creation, for all living things. It doesn't matter if you are an ant, a lion, or a banana slug, you are equally and unconditionally loved, and have a place in the great big circle of life.

But how many of us feel that kind of love - for ourselves and others? I don't mean the conditional love where we only like the best parts of ourselves. I mean deep-down, unconditional love and acceptance of who you are and all that you bring to this world. If we don't really love and value ourselves, how can we follow our heart's song? If it sings to us, we'll just ignore it, and say, "Yeah, that's nice but I have bills to pay and mouths to feed. I've got no time for you."

But if we love and value ourselves, the way Mother Nature does, when we begin to hear our heart's song as a powerful voice, we'll know that it is there to put us on the road to right action. It will clear the way through all our challenges. It will show us both-and, how to live in a world of love and still pay the bills and raise our family. That is the real reason we have to do all this personal healing. It's to come into that place of true, unconditional love. For in that love, a light is turned on inside us. And that light will shine its way to find our connection with ourselves and the Universe.

Acting solely from the heart is one of the hardest things for me, so I appreciate if this all feels a bit uncomfortable. Every action I make my ego wants to speak up and say, "Will it make you money? Will you lose money? Will you get more status? Will you get more views on Instagram?" I am constantly reminding myself that this voice is trying to drive me back down to that place of transactional relationships. This is not yachay or right thinking because it is not based on the ideas of harmony and giving. It is also not based on what my heart wants, which is to help and serve.

A true artist makes art to express what is in their heart. It doesn't matter if one person likes it or one million people like it, only that it is a true and authentic expression of themselves. The rest is up to the Universe.

Finding munay puts us in the right frame of mind. It aligns our thoughts with the bigger picture so that our actions are in ilankay, or right doing. Our actions become harmonious, and we begin to live by the fourth principle of kawsay, living life in harmony. When our hearts, minds, and actions are in harmony, then we begin to live in Ayni, and the universe opens up a world of mutualism and reciprocity. The world starts to take care of us because we are taking care of it.

We develop an awareness of our actions, not doing them like a robot with our hearts and brains turned off. Yes, we need to pay the mortgage.

But we can do this in a way that is in alignment with these principles. We can do it with awareness of how it affects others. We can try to align our hearts and actions into a place of love and giving, not taking. Then we open ourselves up to all the joy and abundance that will come back to us.

\* \* \*

Ever since that dream I had in Peru about living in Ayni, with all the buildings and plants in harmony, I have been asking my heart to show me how to bring that dream into my reality. One of the things that kept coming up for me was healing the land. I live in Colorado, which is a dry state full of mountains and semi-arid plains. Water is a big issue, as is habitat destruction as human development continues to expand.

I've known this as an intellectual problem in my mind, but it wasn't until I felt this in my heart that I moved into a place of right action. I was walking through a park near my house which is very open with tall grasses and a pond in the middle. All winter a coyote family has been wandering the park, even during the day. They've made us humans realize that this park is as much their home as it is a place for our recreation.

After that walk, I had an image come into my mind that guided me into a place of munay, yachay, and ilankay. The image was of a healthy prairie, with tall grasses of every variety, shape, and hue. It was the kind of prairie we can occasionally still find pockets of in Colorado, in between the miles of suburbia or farmland. There were little mice and rabbits, scurrying around under the grasses. A meadowlark perched on the yucca plant, and small birds bounced around in the grasses and short shrubs. A hawk soared overhead and a coyote stalked the fields for prey. Everything was in balance and harmony, just as it should be.

Then all of a sudden, a lush green lawn with a wooden-framed, vinyl-sided house came and plopped itself right there on the prairie. It looked so funny with its pretentious lushness against the pale green-brown of the prairie. The mice and squirrels were interested in the green lawn, but for all the rest of the wildlife, it was an alien landscape to them.

I thought to myself this is what it must have been like as the indigenous people of America watched in horror as colonials 'tamed' the prairie. They took a system that was perfectly in balance, dug it up, and sowed seeds brought from another land. They destroyed the native plants and animals to make way for their familiar food, introducing tons of water to keep these new species alive.

I do not have the power to change the past or shift the entire paradigm, but this vision inspired me to take action in my own corner of the world. I wanted to make things right for the plants and animals around me and to restore what had been destroyed. I started to do a lot of research on re-wilding, especially re-wilding our suburban landscapes with native plantings. Native plants evolved over millennia with the native animals and insects, and by replanting them I could provide both food and homes for many local species. These plants also are adapted to the dry Colorado climate, requiring less water and maintenance than my manicured green lawn.

So this year I'm working on removing my lawn and planting native plants, especially ones that help the local pollinators – the bees and butterflies and hummingbirds. I could say that I was doing this to reduce my water bill which has been going up recently, but that is not why I am doing it. If that was the only reason, I'd choose the hardiest low water plants or go with all gravel. I am specifically picking native plants that can restore habitat. I am doing this out of love for this incredible place I call home and a sincere desire to help it come back into balance. I'm doing it to create homes for the birds and insects so that they have a spot to rest in between the miles of lawns. I realize it is only a small thing, and won't change the course of the world, but I'm doing it anyways because I know it is the right thing to do. This is ilankay, right doing.

To live in Ayni, a place of mutualism and reciprocity, we realize that we are all connected. There is no "they," for we are all just reflections of each other. We are all part of humanity, and humanity is part of this planet. If we can see our own pain reflected in the eyes of others, we can come into a place of genuine love and compassion for our brothers and sisters. Then together, when we are in that place of love and compassionate listening, we can feel into what is needed in this world. We come into a place of right doing, one that is in Ayni.

When we are in Ayni, we can come into the "flow" of life. We begin to feel the cycle of the planet and understand the balance and love that is there. In nature, everything works out as it should without great effort or "doing." When we come back to harmony and balance, our world will also start to move as it should, as we move with it. I spent many months 'thinking' how to heal my corner of the land, but the day I knew what to do it took no effort at all. I just knew. That is the 'flow'. When we are in the flow, we understand that we are a part of everything and then also understand our place in all of that. Our ideas and our actions will all come naturally from the heart, from that quiet voice inside. The world around us begins to flow as it should, for the betterment of all living things.

* * *

# AYNI

\*\*\*

# 15

## Finding your Brave

*"Be sure you put your feet in the right place, then stand firm"*
*– Abraham Lincoln*

When talking to friends about how we can make the world a better place, the biggest challenge I've found is the feeling that we alone can't change the tide. That it's all just too big, that everything is just too broken, and we feel helpless as we watch the horror unfold. We become paralyzed at the enormity of everything that is wrong, so don't even know where to start.

I want to share a dream I had about a wave. I often dream of big waves, the kind they would put in an apocalypse movie that's coming for the entire town. They used to terrify me in my dreams, and I would always wake up before they came to destroy me and everything around me. After my trip to the Sacred Valley in Peru, my dreams shifted. Then the waves came to offer me wisdom.

\* \* \*

# The Wave

*I stand in front of the ocean, and it looks deceptively calm. Many people are around, laughing and smiling. It's a happy beach scene. I wade into the water, still holding all my possessions -my towel, my clothes, and my phone - in one hand. I realize this is odd, but I can't find a place to put them with all the people around.*

*As soon as I get comfortable, waist deep in the sea, a giant wave comes out of nowhere. It is as tall as a building and just beginning to crest. I know I have to choose in that moment. How important are my possessions? I can waste precious time trying to secure them on the shore, or I can just let them go. I know I have no time. I have to go out to greet the wave before it comes crashing onto me. I have to go forward into the deep to dive under the surf. Running away from the wave would only guarantee getting caught in the washout.*

*So, I let go of my possessions, casting them aside. I run forward toward the wave. And I dive. I dive deep to the very root where all is still, so I can avoid the turbulence above. And in that stillness, I feel the wave wash over me, pass me by. Then I woke up.*

\* \* \*

Courage does not mean that you are not scared, but that you face the fear and move forward anyway. That's what I did in my dream. I let go of my possessions and swam forward to face the wave, to greet it, and then went deep. Deep into the ocean, deep into my shadows, and in that space I found stillness. Peace. Serenity. And all the turbulence above was just noise, as I swam through the deep ocean. And when I woke up I knew that somewhere out there someone else was also facing their own wave. So, I share its wisdom. Be courageous, dive deep, and you will make it through to the other side.

We have all seen bravery and felt those moments of bravery in our own lives. For me, I have felt brave most often when standing up for those I love. I can go to the bat for my child, my partner, or even a stranger I see being mistreated. Bravery is so closely linked to love. That which we love is that which we will stand up for. In some cases could give our lives for.

But when was the last time you found bravery for yourself? For asking for that promotion you knew you deserved, that seat at the table in the business meeting, or in giving yourself time and space for personal health, mental or physical? When was the last time you gave yourself permission to speak your truth or follow your passion? When was the last time you went to the bat for YOU? When was the last time you even thought about what it was you wanted to go to the bat for? If we can find bravery for that which we love, why is it so hard to find bravery for ourselves? Is it because, still after all this time, we struggle with loving and valuing ourselves?

Why is it so hard to find our own brave? Why do we still feel powerless in the world, watching the horrors of climate change, poverty, inequity, and war unfold? How can we come to this place of Ayni when we feel helpless against the great wave that is crashing down all around us?

In my quietest moments, I hear the answer, and the answer is LOVE. That which we love is that which we will stand up for. Do we love ourselves? Do we love each other? Do we love the planet? If we do, if we really do in our heart of hearts, we will find our brave.

\* \* \*

## Practice: Finding Your Brave

I invite you to take a moment and sit quietly for a few breaths. Maybe practice the 4-4-4-4 breath for 2 minutes.

Now, write down what is your innermost heart's desire, what you would want to find the courage to stand up for, and what it is that is calling you to find your brave. If you don't know what that is at first, take another minute to listen. Listen until you hear that small quiet voice inside you, the one that speaks from your heart.

And then, taking a few more deep breaths, ask yourself, what is holding you back? And write that down. Now ask yourself, are you ready to let that limiting belief go? Are you ready to find your brave? If so, bring it to the fire. Hold a fire ceremony. Offer that limiting belief to the fire, by blowing it into a toothpick or writing it on a piece of paper. Ask the fire to transform it, and to give you the wisdom so you can find your right action, the one that comes from your heart.

What is your innermost desire?

What limiting belief is holding you back from achieving it?

\* \* \*

## Finding your Super Strength

If you find that heart's desire, that which you are willing to fight for, then the next step is one of action. And to be really powerful in our actions we need to find our super strength.

For about as long as I can remember, I've always gotten passionate about doing what is right for each other and the planet. I didn't know the word Ayni, but when I finally learned about it, I just KNEW, this was it. This was my passion. This was my dream—that we could come together and live in a place of giving, trust, and love.

Of course, whenever I talked about this passion, in architectural school, my various jobs, or with my friends, I was usually called out as idealistic and a bit naïve. And so, like so many things, it went underground, into the shadows. I felt powerless to create the change that I wanted to see in the world, and even in myself.

I became one of the many people who looked at the unfolding climate crisis and felt powerless to stop it. I would bring up my desire to create net zero buildings (making as much energy as they are using) at my State architectural job but was always told the budget was a higher priority. We had to reduce budgets, not increase them. We can't do anything unless we can get more money, more resources, more time. We need more, more, more. Even though the government would create mandates, the government agencies were not given the funds to comply with them.

I was watching a train wreck unfolding but had been given the message from a very young age that I alone can't change the tide. It's just too big, what can one person do? If the governments can't agree on a plan forward, then what can we as citizens do? We just feel helpless and lost. Climate change related depression and anxiety are very real things.

One of my super strengths (or curses), is that I am incredibly stubborn.

My father, who is Finnish, told me they have a word for it in Finland. It's called "Sisu." It essentially means stoic determination, that no matter what happens, we keep going. I called on it when I was running my first marathon, and I called on it whenever I get really down about climate change. While I was powerless in my job to affect change, it did not diminish my desire to do so. I tried again and again and met brick wall after brick wall. But I couldn't give up. And so I quit that job. I said I'd rather not design buildings at all than design ones that hurt the environment. But it wasn't really quitting. It was creating space for a shift. Seeing that something wasn't working and allowing myself to find something that did work, that was more in alignment with my heart.

And of course, that is not the end of the story. My stoic determination is still guiding me. First, I am writing this book in the hope to inspire and build a community of people wanting to live in Ayni. I will make changes in my own life, like replanting my yard with native plants, having an electric car, and subscribing to renewable energy. I will also keep trying to find clients that are interested in healing themselves and the environment, whether through architecture, yoga, or shamanism. The story will continue, because I don't ever give up.

I will admit, at the time when I turned in my resignation, a big part of me felt angry and defeated, that I was too weak and small to make any change. And so I get it. I get that feeling of we can't do anything.

But as I've been on this journey, as I've personally been working on my shadows and on self-love, I've also been working on my relationship with power. My own power – finding it and understanding it. I didn't have the power at that job to affect change, but that did not mean I was powerless, it just meant my power was not there. I had other powers – superpowers.

Besides my stubbornness, my other superpowers are listening and building consensus. My great skills are planning and problem solving.

And my super strengths are my passion, my empathy, and my desire to nurture and love. These are not weaknesses or liabilities like I once thought, but strengths to nurture. And I can use these superpowers to live in Ayni and help others as well.

I can use these skills to hear from different arguing groups and help them find a path forward of peace and harmony. I can use my super strength of compassion and empathy to be a powerful healer, to nurture and love. I can use my love of writing and communication to write this book.

What are your superpowers? Are you great at logistics? Are you a wonderful communicator or writer? Are you good with your hands? Are you a great cheerleader, supporting others? Are you a profound listener? Are you stubborn and determined?

* * *

## Practice: What are Your Superpowers?

Take a moment and really think about this question. Now, write these things down. Don't write down what you wish you were good at, write down what you are good at. Don't be shy, these are gifts. These are true treasures that you can and should use to live your highest purpose. I believe that each of us is unique and blessed with different gifts because that is the way the Universe works. Just like the four feathers taught us there are so many kinds of birds on the planet, each with its own place, each of us has our own gifts that we can share with the world.

What are your superpowers, your unique gifts?
1.
2.

3.

4.

Now, look at your gifts, really look at them, and see them for what they are? These are your superpowers! They could even be that you're good at making money or running a business. These gifts were given to you, for this moment. Out of the entire Universe, you were given those gifts. Don't take that for granted!

Now, ask yourself, how are you using your superpowers?

Be honest here. Are you using them to further the story of fear and scarcity? The story of "every man for himself?" The story of being a taker? It's okay, remember, there is no judgment here, just love. Write down whatever comes to your mind.

Now ask yourself, how would you like to use your superpowers? Imagine you are a kid again and someone gave you a cloak and shield and told you that you had these amazing gifts. Then they ask you, "What will you do with them?" Now, answer that someone honestly.

Okay, so here's the big question. Are the two in alignment? Is the answer you would have given as a child, what you are doing with those gifts today? If so, that's amazing! Keep it up! If not, that's okay, too! You have been living in the story that we've all been told of scarcity and fear, not love and abundance. Like so many of us, the dreams you had as a child have been pushed down as you've been told to conform.

But, what if? What if you used those gifts for the betterment of all living things? What if you used those gifts to help all of us live in Ayni? What would that look like? Ask yourself, what, if anything would you want to change?

We are a world of eight billion people with every gift imaginable. The question is what to do with these gifts.

If you're wonderful with logistics planning, could you use that gift to help eliminate food waste? More than 100 billion pounds of food is wasted in America each year and yet 34 million Americans are food insecure. We can fix that!

If you're good with plants and landscaping, could you use that skill to help people design sustainable plantings with native plants? Can you help educate people about why it's good to do so?

Are you a great networker? What if you used that superpower to connect people with others who needed a little help with a meal or job skill training?

I know each of you has your thing, your dream, your passion, and your superpower. And I also bet that each of you has been told to conform and fall into line with the paradigm of the Taker. Some of you have already broken out of that paradigm, but some, like me, are still struggling to break free.

I come back, again and again, to the idea of a pebble in a sea of pebbles. A blade of grass in an endless meadow. Though we are small, we are mighty. And if each of us uses our superpower for good, for the betterment of all living things, then we will change the face of the Earth. If each of us gives of ourselves, freely, without expectation, then we will break the paradigm. We will come into Ayni.

For if we all do it, then we will receive ten times what we give out. But if we all hold our superpowers in and only use them for ourselves, then we will never receive anything back.

# AYNI

**\* \* \***

# 16

# Action from the Heart

*"The Creation of a thousand forests is in one acorn."*
*-Ralph Waldo Emerson*

Now that you have found your superpowers, what to do with them?
Let me start this chapter with another dream I had. This past summer I spent a week at a yoga retreat in Whistler, British Columbia. I spent all week with my Swami from Australia, communing with old growth forests and alpine lakes, practicing deep yoga meditations, and trying to find out how I fit into the world. The last night I was there, I had a dream...about Brad Pitt.

\* \* \*

*In my dream, Brad Pitt was standing at the front of a big crowd, talking, laughing, and carrying on. Everyone was enraptured by him, because, well, he's Brad Pitt!*

*He came up to me and started to become quite inappropriate and a little naughty. I didn't have any idea what to do and was standing there completely speechless. My Swami came up to him and was inappropriate and naughty right back. It felt quite scandalous but also hilarious. She completely put him in his place. Then she walked away and disappeared from the dream.*

*Once she was gone, bombs started to fall from the sky. I thought to myself, "Good for her. She knew just when to leave, but now what do I do?"*

*Then all of a sudden Brad Pitt reappeared, driving a big school bus. But now he was changed. He was not naughty or inappropriate. He was serious and helpful. He was there to help me and my family onto the bus so that we could escape the bombs and make it through the war. He led us through explosions, through mazes and landmines, and through so many other struggles, keeping us safe and protected.*

* * *

When I woke up, I asked Swamiji what the dream meant. She said, "Well it is quite obvious to me, but maybe not to you." And she explained. Brad Pitt represented my ego. Swami represented my Higher Self. I had been listening to my ego, but it's naughty and acts up and can't be relied upon. It was in control but wasn't taking me anywhere I wanted to be. From a place of higher authority, my Higher Self could talk its language and put it in its right place, a place of service. Then when the difficulties in life come (the bombs in my dream) the ego can help us through these difficulties. It can act in concert with our higher self and not in opposition. The ego just needs to understand that it isn't in charge, it's only driving the bus. My Swami left me in the dream because I didn't need her anymore. When my higher self and my ego were in alignment, I had everything I needed within me to navigate life's difficulties and fulfill my highest destiny. My outer guru had helped me find my inner guru.

I can tell you from personal experience that the more I listen to my intuition, the more I am in tune with the bigger picture, and the easier it is to come into balance and harmony. The more I put ego into a path of service, the more it falls in line with the overall plan of the Universe. As I have cultivated my higher wisdom's voice, the obstacles that I perceived to be there have melted away, and my path to Ayni has opened up before me. I have found that my intuition, my higher mind, has a direct path to the even higher wisdom, the wisdom of the planet. We do not need to look outside of ourselves for the answers, the answer is within us all along. We only need to listen. We need to listen to our intuition, and to our heart.

But then, life comes along and stirs us up again. I leave the yoga retreat and get back into the daily grind. My ego, my mind, takes control again, and I immediately go back into "Doing" mode and not "Being" mode. As soon as I get back into the thick of daily life, I want to go back to acting from the mind and not the heart. And so, even when I came to what I found were my "superpowers," my first instinct was to act on them from my mind. I start writing flurries of emails, calling up organizations, and spreading myself out as far and wide as my mind could imagine. But that was acting from the ego and not from the heart, and so they were not nearly as productive as when I just stopped for a minute and let my heart guide me.

Earlier I talked about the five principles of living in the Incan and Andean culture. The first was munay, or love. Acting from a place of love. That's why we went on the journey of loving ourselves and coming into a loving place with others, so that we could begin to flex that heart muscle. Maybe for some, this is natural, but for many of us, we are very much caught up in our minds and our doing. We do not know how to sit still, to "be," to listen to what our hearts have to say.

Our minds ask us "Why?" Why not use the brain to solve the problems of the climate crisis? What does the heart have to show us? We can invent our way out of this problem. We can build a colony on the Moon and use technology to sequester carbon. We can use more chemical engineering to create new plastics that biodegrade. We can create a metaverse so we don't care if the planet falls apart around us. But be careful—this is the mind again taking charge. It is that loud annoying voice that just throws out 100 ideas to see what sticks. It will spin out ideas left and right, saying it knows the best way. But the mind is the driver, not the map. Like my dream about Brad Pitt, our problem-solving minds are a great tool, but they can't be the ones making the maps. The heart makes the map, and the mind drives the bus.

So first, before we act, we must listen. Yes, we see the problem, and we see our gifts, and we may see some solutions, but we must listen to what the Universe has to say about it, too. We must listen to the wind, to the rivers, and the fish in them. We must ask them how we can heal this broken world. We must not assume we have all the answers.

The other day I sat outside on a beautiful sunny day. I put my hands on the ground, feeling into the energy of Mother Earth. I asked her, "What can we do to start healing you? What can we do to start healing the world?" And she gave me her answer. It was two words, and they were as clear and as strong as any message I've ever received. She said, "Stop Fighting."

That's it. I had chapters in this book written about the actions I wanted to take to reduce our carbon footprints, to reduce, reuse and recycle, and to 'do no harm' in my building practices. But I took all of them out for the final edit. Why? Because Pachamama told me that none of that matters right now. The only thing that matters, the only thing I'm supposed to say to all of us, is "Stop Fighting." Then, maybe we can move on to some of those other actions.

But that is my message from Her and my call to action. I invite you to do a practice where you listen to your own heart. Where you ask the Universe how best to use your gifts. Where you ask what your roadmap should look like. Just as I asked Mother Earth to "show me" how to best help heal her, I invite you to ask Spirit or the Universe the same thing.

* * *

## Practice: Acting from Your Heart

Find a comfortable and quiet place to sit. If it's nice outside and you can sit on the Earth or be in nature, even better, but anywhere is fine. What is most important is that you will not be disturbed for a short while. Bring up a feeling of intention, an intention to ask questions of your heart and your deeper intuition.

Take a few deep grounding breaths. Then Practice the 4-4-4-4 breath. Inhale to the count of four, hold to the count of four, exhale to the count of four, and hold to the count of four. Continue this eight times or about two minutes. Then let go of the counting and take another deep inhale and exhale. Now, with your eyes closed, imagine you are standing in a beautiful meadow. Visualize yourself in that meadow. Feel the sun shining down on you, feel the grass beneath your feet. Notice if there are any plants or animals around you. Feel safe, supported, and peaceful in that meadow. Look around and take in all that you see in your mind's eye. Then, looking ahead in the meadow, see a great big beautiful tree, the tree of life. Now start to walk to that tree. As you get closer to the tree notice there is a big boulder in front of the tree, a perfect size and shape for sitting on. Imagine you are walking over to that boulder. Sit down on the rock, feel its coolness. And as you sit there, ask in your mind, "What do balance and harmony feel like to me?" Just listen, see if the answer comes. See if any images come, if there's any feelings in your body, or if there is a voice speaking to you in your mind. Notice if the voice in your head is the loud voice of the ego or the quiet voice of your intuition. If it is the ego, then wait a little longer, and give intuition a chance to speak.

Now ask yourself, "What gifts do I have that could help me create that place of balance and harmony?" Listen quietly. Give yourself time to see or hear whatever comes to mind.

Now ask a third question. "What should I do with my gifts? How can I act from the heart?" Listen again. Notice whatever comes up. Listen for any messages or images that come to you. Notice if anyone or anything comes to offer you guidance. If you feel the need to ask for them, you can call them in. Call in your angel or spirit guide to help you find the answer.

Then, when you have received your answers, stand up from the boulder. Bow in gratitude to the boulder, to the great tree beyond the boulder, to this place of nature within. Bow in gratitude to your inner voice and your spirit guides if they helped you today. Walk back through the meadow, coming back to your own body. Take a few deep breaths and come back to your surroundings. Take a moment and journal whatever messages you received.

* * *

# 17

# The Circle

*To see a World in a Grain of Sand*
*And a Heaven in a Wild Flower,*
*Hold Infinity in the palm of your hand*
*And Eternity in an hour.*
*—William Blake*

In Western cultures, we look at time as a line—past-present-future. In shamanic cultures, they look at time as a circle. It wraps on itself like an endless Möbius strip.

The past, the present, and the future weave back and forth. The shaman can step out of time and heal the past or guide the future.

Like that Möbius strip, our relationship to ourselves, to each other, and to the planet also fold back and forth on each other. We are interconnected and interrelated. Our past, present, and future are also connected, and the future can be changed by our actions today. And as we make a change individually, it begins to affect others. We can heal one piece of the great puzzle, and the other pieces also start to heal. This is the true interconnectedness of everything. Time, space, energy, it is all weaving together in an endless circle.

What we do today affects the future; it is not pre-ordained. People theorize about what could happen if we went back in the past and made a small change, how it would cascade into the present and create all sorts of new possible timelines or Universes. That theory applies to today, too. What if we make one small change today? Could that not also cascade into endless possible futures? The shamans of the Andes looked into the future and saw a healed world, and then brought it back to our present to give us a roadmap to that destiny. That roadmap is to live in right relationship with the Earth and each other, to live in Ayni. We only have to choose to walk it.

My journey to living in Ayni started from a place of healing myself. It was only in finding self-love that could I find the courage and conviction to walk fully in my path. We can also come to this path from a place of service, like the yoga eightfold path offered by Swami Sivananda. In the process of service, we heal ourselves and others. It doesn't matter which end we start at because it's all a circle. Our actions can heal our hearts, just as a healed heart can inform our actions.

No matter what path we choose, it is about intention. What is our intention? What is our heart's desire? And what gifts do we have to help us get there?

My intention is to live in Ayni. To give freely without expectation and to offer love and light to whoever needs it. My heart's desire is to live in harmony with all our relations and to walk the path of an Earth Keeper. I invite you to find your intention, your heart's desire, and then the courage and conviction to follow it no matter where it takes you.

To live in Ayni is to acknowledge that we are all related, what one of us does affects the other. All of creation – the plants and animals, the rocks, the oceans, and the stars in the sky – we are all in a circle. All eight billion of us humans are as interconnected as the fungi in the soil are with the trees and plants. All the birds in the sky are connected with the stars and the magnetic pull of the Earth. What we do matters.

Not only does what we do matter, it matters to the entire cosmos.

There is so much responsibility in that statement, but also so much beauty. Beauty that we can live in a world that dances to the songs of the stars and is full of bounty. Responsibility because we make that choice in every action we do.

So, we choose what we do wisely and with intention, for who knows what ripple effect it will have. If our words and actions are from our hearts, they will guide us back to Pachamama, to Mother Earth. They will lead us to a beautiful garden of love and abundance. If they are always from the ego, then they will keep us in a place of fear and scarcity.

And so, I ask you, dear reader, would you like to live in Ayni? Would you like to live in right relationship with yourself, each other, and the planet? Would you like to hear once again the whisper of the wind and the messages of the songbird? Mother Nature is not broken. She is full of life, wisdom, and love. If we can listen to her again and begin to live in harmony with her song, we will also be full of life, wisdom, and love.

It is not easy to change things, but it is worth trying. Our lives are short, and we are just a pebble in a sea of pebbles, but our ability to influence is far greater than we know. It only takes a spark.

\* \* \*

# AYNI

\* \* \*

# 18

# Conclusion

If you're interested in learning more about any of the things I talked about in the book here are some references.

**Websites for my Yoga and Shamanic Lineages and Teachers**

- Four Winds Institute https://thefourwinds.com/
- Bihar School of Yoga https://www.biharyoga.net/
- Bihar School's Yoga Magazine: Free Magazine with thoughtful articles http://yogamag.net/
- My Yoga Swami's website: https://yoga-with-muktibodha.info/
- Link to P.J. Sanderson's Book: https://www.goodreads.com/book/show/56345131-the-bird-of-destiny
- Shamanic Teacher Karen Johnson's Website **https://karenjohnson.net/**
- Shamanic Teacher Peter Sanderson's YouTube Channel https://www.youtube.com/@sandep10
- My Youtube Channel https://www.youtube.com/@Elucero108

## References from the Book

- Full Transcript of President Zelenskyy's Speech https://www.nyti mes.com/2022/12/21/us/politics/zelensky-speech-transcript.ht ml
- Article about Emotions vs Feelings https://counseling.online.wfu. edu/blog/difference-feelings-emotions/
- Article on Swami Sivinanda's Eight Fold Path http://www.yogam ag.net/archives/2000s/2005/0509/0509assv.html
- Links to Yoga Nidra
- https://open.spotify.com/album/00Dzgh60bmNigM9fvckKa3
- https://www.youtube.com/watch?v=zULPcwATVl0
- https://www.youtube.com/watch?v=R2GRhAFplkI
- https://www.youtube.com/watch?v=jPTRzOxmbZ8
- HeatherAsh Amara's Website is https://warriorgoddess.com/
- The time of the Pachacuti https://adishakti.org/_/prophecies_of_ the_qero_inca_shamans.htm
- More on Corbin Harney https://www.pbs.org/circleofstories/sto rytellers/corbin_harney.html
- Indigenous people protecting Biodiversity https://www.worldw ildlife.org/stories/recognizing-indigenous-peoples-land-interes ts-is-critical-for-people-and-nature#:~:text=Although%20they% 20comprise%20less%20than,they%20have%20lived%20for%20ce nturies
- United Nations Summit and Indigenous participation https://w ww.cbc.ca/news/science/indigenous-nations-status-cop15-1.66 81705
- An article about Ayni https://drjewilliams.com/wp-content/uplo ads/2014/12/Five-Principles_PositiveChangeAp07-copy-1.pdf

I was called to take out a few chapters in my final edit about things that I or others are doing to reduce our impact on the planet and begin to heal our relationship with the earth. If you are interested in reading more about these, here are several references that inspire me daily.

- Colorado Native Plant Society https://conps.org/
- Native Plants List by State https://nativebackyards.com/native-plants-by-state/
- The Interdependence of Species in the American West https://earthjustice.org/blog/2015-july/how-wolves-saved-the-foxes-mice-and-rivers-of-yellowstone-national-park
- Sustainable Fish Ponds in Hawaii https://thecounter.org/native-hawaiians-ancient-fishponds-revival-food-sovereignty-pandemic/
- Food Carbon Footprint https://www.greeneatz.com/foods-carbon-footprint.html#:~:text=A%20vegan%20diet%20has%20the,of%20a%20meat%2Dlover's%20diet.
- Our Fashion Footprint https://www.liveabout.com/textile-recycling-facts-and-figures-2878122
- Size of American Homes over the Years https://compasscaliforniablog.com/have-american-homes-changed-much-over-the-years-take-a-look/
- Reducing Food Waste https://www.feedingamerica.org/our-work/reduce-food-waste#:~:text=Each%20year%2C%20119%20billion%20pounds,food%20in%20America%20is%20wasted.

AYNI

\* \* \*

# Epilogue

## Return to the Source

Fast forward 1,000 years, 10,000 years, what does Planet Earth look like? That is what an epilogue is for in a book, to take the characters into the future, and to help us imagine their fate. Since we are all the characters in this book, what is our collective future?

As I finished writing this book, I had a powerful meditation. It was a call to look backward to understand how things will unfold in the future. It was a call to visit the Ancient Ones.

\* \* \*

*I'm on the edge of a sandy cliff, with the water far below. My husband is sitting on the beach with me, along with others, sitting in comfort and enjoying the sunshine. I see young people slide down the sandy cliff and into the water, but don't see how they get back up again. I see cars being driven off the edge, crashing into the water below, with their music still blaring, and somehow even as they sink the people are smiling and laughing in the water. But those of us on the beach feel it is better to stay up here, where it's comfortable and safe.*

*Then the dreamscape shifts, and I hear the ancient ones call me to take the leap. At first, I'm not sure if they are here to teach me to fly, or to meet me under the water. But either way, they are calling me to face my fear. I must jump. But I'm afraid. I try to feel into it, sit with it, and work through it. It's not fear of dying, as I have seen others have survived the leap. It is the fear of the unknown. It is the fear of leaving the comfort behind, and maybe not being able to come back to it. It is the fear that jumping off the cliff may leave my old life behind. As I sit in this meditation, two of my dogs are sitting at my feet and lick my hands. It is almost like they are encouraging me, telling me I must do this. For them, for our future.*

*Everything stops. Time, movement, space; I am suspended in the air for a moment. The fear evaporates and I am in a moment of stillness before I dive down into the depths of the water.*

*There, underneath the water, are the ancient whales waiting to greet me. I had been dreaming about them for the last few weeks. They would lay at the edge of the water, beckoning me to come out, but in every dream I had there was something holding me back. They are long dark creatures, with small fins and tails, distant relatives of the whales of today, but I knew, instinctively, they hold the secrets of the ancient wisdom. They were the ancient ones that had been calling to me. Underneath the waves they show me how to breathe, to swim with them, so that I could see the secrets of the ancient ocean.*

*What they showed me as I swam with them was a mixture of ideas and symbols, and I will try my best to translate them into words.*

*In the ancient seas, things evolved together, for mutual benefit. It was not just the Darwin idea of survival of the fittest, though of course, that happened. Evolution created ever-expanding relationships and harmonies. As we swam they showed me the plants, the fish, and the whales as they grew, fed, and cared for each other. Evolution was not just survival. It was the source creating diversity, spreading out from a single source to a multitude of beings, which grew and thrived dependent on each other. I saw a spiral, like a whirlpool, but in reverse. The single source spun outward and outward as life grew. It was a circle, ever-expanding, as the world and all its species expanded. I asked if they could show me the future, the future of all things, the destiny of our world. We went inside the whirlpool, and it opened like a tunnel or wormhole. I went forward, through the tunnel, into the future, and I felt the whirlpool swirling, swirling back inward, back to the source. The future was about coming back together, back to the source. All of creation - the earth, the humans, the plants, and the animals - were all a part of that spiral, and it was spiraling back in.*

*It was not that species biodiversity was shrinking back to fewer beings, though that may happen during this time. What it felt like, was that the spiral was almost like all our collective DNA; and all our collective species and diversity would become re-connected. That we would no longer be expanding outwards, as we had for millennia, but would be coming back inwards. The time of expanding diversity had ended, and we would now be coming back into one organism. As that one organism, we might still be many individuals, but we would also be a part of the collective whole.*

*We would know and understand what the other creatures needed. We would be in sync with them again, as we were in the ancient oceans when all of life was new and fragile and needed each other to survive. I saw a time when humanity was more than what they are now, when their minds spoke to each other and also to the birds and wolves. When we were the source, and the source was us.*

*And as I viewed this collective destiny, I felt myself in that swirl. The swirl of everything mixing together, creating, dying, transforming, coming together.*

*I thanked the Ancient Ones for this vision, who brought into understanding where we are within the great spiral. We are at the point where things start to come back together again. And many people, creatures, and other things may be lost as this happens. We have expanded as far as creation allows, and now we must come back together, back into harmony. As this happens, there will be loss, but that loss can guide us to feel into the source. We can feel the source in each life, in each species, that is lost to the great circle. It will help us find the source within those that remain. And that will help us come back into the One.*

*I came back up to the surface of the water, and I was out at sea, with no idea where that cliff was. I had no idea where land was. But it was okay now because I had learned how to breathe under the water. I had learned how to swim with the ancient ones. I trusted that everything would be as it should.*

\* \* \*

# About the Author

Erin Lucero graduated with honors from Rensselaer Polytechnic Institute with a Bachelor of Architecture and a minor in communications and has had a lifelong love of writing and creative expression. She is an author, practicing architect, shamanic healer, and yoga practitioner. She considers herself an Earth keeper and cares deeply for the planet, making it a better place for all living things. She lives in Colorado with her husband, three dogs, and chickens. She loves running, hiking, gardening, and spending as much time as she can in nature.

**You can connect with me on:**
◉ https://www.bladeofgrasshealingarts.com

# Also by Erin Lucero

Erin Lucero writes messages of love, joy, kindness and a little bit of magic for all ages.

### Hudson and the Magic Crow

Hudson is a kind and thoughtful little boy who lives on a farm with his horse, goats, chickens, and lots of dogs. One special day he meets a magical crow who shows him how to fly.

Together, they see the world through the eyes of the crow and learn just how big an impact humans have on the world around them. Hudson learns how he can help the crow and all the plants and animals in nature, and make it a happier place for all the living things.

### Quest for the Phoenix

When Tori saw what she thought was a garden gnome in her backyard, little did she guess the adventures that would await her. Armed with kindness, compassion, and a few funny jokes, this young girl sets out on the quest of a lifetime – to help the magical phoenix be reborn, and prevent the world from falling into darkness. She travels underground rivers, meets magical creatures, and overcomes great obstacles in her quest for the phoenix. Along the way, Tori will also discover just how much magic she has inside herself, and if a single young girl can save the entire world.